EARNESTLY
CONTEND
FOR THE FAITH

CLARENCE SEXTON

EARNESTLY CONTEND
FOR THE FAITH

CLARENCE SEXTON

SECOND EDITION

COPYRIGHT

NOVEMBER 2004

CROWN
CHRISTIAN
PUBLICATIONS
Royal Reading

1700 BEAVER CREEK DRIVE
POWELL, TENNESSEE ♦ 37849

1-877 AT CROWN
FaithfortheFamily.com

SUNDAY SCHOOL SERIES

EARNESTLY CONTEND FOR THE FAITH

Copyright © 2004
Crown Christian Publications
Powell, Tennessee 37849
ISBN: 1-58981-048-1
Layout and design by Stephen Troell

Printed in the United States of America

DEDICATION

To the students of Crown College, whose time has come to take their stand for the Lord Jesus Christ.

CONTENTS

"Jude, the servant of Jesus Christ, and brother of James, to them that are sanctified by God the Father, and preserved in Jesus Christ, and called."

Jude 1

AN INTRODUCTION TO THE BOOK OF JUDE

 here are twenty-seven books in the New Testament. The first four books are Gospel records—the Gospel according to Matthew, Mark, Luke, and John. Following the Gospel records we come to the book of Acts, sometimes referred to as the Acts of the Apostles. The book of Acts deals with the continuing Christ in the Person of the Holy Spirit working through the lives of the apostles and other followers of the Lamb.

If we view the book of Acts as the book that deals with the beginning of the church age and the work of the apostles as they were empowered by the indwelling Holy Spirit, let us view the book of Jude as the book dealing with the end of the church age and the work of the apostates, those who are empowered by the Devil, turning from revealed truth, yet maintaining an appearance of belief. This book of Jude concerns itself with the acts of the apostates.

Some of the powerful statements given to us in the book of Jude demand special consideration.

Verse 1	*"the servant of Jesus Christ"*
Verse 3	*"the common salvation"*

Verse 3	*"earnestly contend for the faith"*
Verse 3	*"the faith which was once delivered unto the saints"*
Verse 6	*"the judgment of the great day"*
Verse 11	*"the way of Cain"*
Verse 11	*"the error of Balaam"*
Verse 11	*"the gainsaying of Core"*
Verse 13	*"the blackness of darkness for ever"*
Verse 16	*"having men's persons in admiration because of advantage"*
Verse 18	*"should be mockers in the last time"*
Verse 20	*"praying in the Holy Ghost"*
Verse 21	*"Keep yourselves in the love of God"*
Verse 22	*"And of some have compassion, making a difference"*
Verse 23	*"pulling them out of the fire"*
Verse 24	*"him that is able to keep you from falling"*
Verse 25	*"the only wise God our Saviour"*

The book of Jude will help us to come to an understanding of the term *apostate*. Declaring that I am a Christian means I have asked the Lord Jesus Christ to forgive my sin and by faith received Jesus Christ as Savior. Salvation is *"repentance toward God, and faith toward our Lord Jesus Christ"* (Acts 20:21). I am seeking to live my life by the truth of God's Word.

An apostate is someone who has turned from revealed truth. An apostate stands back from the truth. Apostasy is a subtle rejection of essentials while maintaining the outward form of belief. An apostate is not a Christian. An apostate is not someone who is saved and then loses his salvation, because that is an impossibility. The Lord saves us and keeps us saved. An apostate looks at revealed truth; he is not acting in ignorance. He sees the truth, he knows the message of truth, and he turns from it.

The book of Jude forms a vestibule or hallway leading into the book of the Revelation of Jesus Christ. When we come to the Revelation of Jesus Christ, we know that, according to Revelation 1:19, we are dealing with things past, things present, and things to come.

Most of the Revelation of Jesus Christ is devoted to the Tribulation period. The Tribulation period is the seven-year period between the rapture of the church and the revelation of Jesus Christ. At the end of the Tribulation, Christ is coming with ten thousands of His saints to execute judgment upon this unbelieving world. The Lord Jesus Christ is coming for His church before the Tribulation.

We are not to look for signs, but rather for the Savior. Christ is coming again. Our hope is not in the Second Coming of Christ, but in the Christ of the Second Coming. Believe it, teach it, and preach it. His return is imminent; it is at hand. He could come at any moment for His own, but the world will not come to an end. The lost will be left on the earth to go through the Tribulation. The Antichrist will make his appearing when the church is gone.

The book of Jude, this hallway leading into the Revelation of Jesus Christ, is God's way of leading us to the teaching of the "last things" we find in the Bible.

The church age had a beginning. The church started with Christ and His disciples and was empowered at Pentecost. The church age had a beginning, and it also has an ending.

As we read through the twenty-five verses of the book of Jude, we find that God deals with a *duty* and a *danger*. The duty we learn about in verse three, *"Beloved, when I gave all diligence to write unto you of the common salvation, it was needful for me to write unto you, and exhort you that ye should earnestly contend for the faith which was once delivered unto the saints."* It is our duty to *"earnestly contend for the faith."*

> *Apostasy is a subtle rejection of essentials while maintaining the outward form of belief.*

The great danger we face is found in verse four, *"For there are certain men crept in unawares, who were before of old ordained to this condemnation, ungodly men, turning the grace of our God into lasciviousness, and denying the only Lord God, and our Lord Jesus Christ."*

We are living in days of darkness, saturated with doctrines of demons. This is a time of apostasy. May God help us to proclaim the truth.

There is coming a great falling away. We read about this falling away in I Timothy 4:1, *"Now the Spirit speaketh expressly, that in the latter times some shall depart from the faith, giving heed to seducing spirits, and doctrines of devils."*

The Bible says in II Timothy 4:1-4,

> *I charge thee therefore before God, and the Lord Jesus Christ, who shall judge the quick and*

the dead at his appearing and his kingdom; preach the word; be instant in season, out of season; reprove, rebuke, exhort with all longsuffering and doctrine. For the time will come when they will not endure sound doctrine; but after their own lusts shall they heap to themselves teachers, having itching ears; and they shall turn away their ears from the truth, and shall be turned unto fables.

God said that there is coming a time when people would rather hear a lie than hear the truth. Note what God gives us in II Peter 2:1-2,

But there were false prophets also among the people, even as there shall be false teachers among you, who privily shall bring in damnable heresies, even denying the Lord that bought them, and bring upon themselves swift destruction. And many shall follow their pernicious ways; by reason of whom the way of truth shall be evil spoken of.

The Word of God teaches that many people will follow the damnable heresies taught by false teachers. In II Peter 3:1-3 the Bible says,

This second epistle, beloved, I now write unto you; in both which I stir up your pure minds by way of remembrance: that ye may be mindful of the words which were spoken before by the holy prophets, and of the commandment of us the apostles of the Lord and Saviour: knowing this first, that there shall come in the last days scoffers, walking after their own lusts.

These scoffers have always existed, but we are living in an intense time of scoffing. The Bible says that the reason they scoff is that they are walking after their own lusts. They would rather have people say that they are right than say that God is right.

There are twenty-five verses in this book. The first verse says, *"Jude, the servant of Jesus Christ, and brother of James, to them that are sanctified by God the Father, and preserved in Jesus Christ, and called."*

THE BIRTH OF THIS SERVANT

This letter begins with the identity of the person who is writing. When we receive letters, we look at the end of the letter to find who wrote it.

The human author of this letter is a man named Jude. This particular Jude says of himself that he is the servant (this word means *"bondslave"*) of Jesus Christ. The Bible says in Matthew 13:53-55,

> *And it came to pass, that when Jesus had finished these parables, he departed thence. And when he was come into his own country, he taught them in their synagogue, insomuch that they were astonished, and said, Whence hath this man this wisdom, and these mighty works? is not this the carpenter's son? is not his mother called Mary? and his brethren, James, and Joses, and Simon, and Judas?*

The name *Jude* we find in our English Bible is the same word as *Judas*. It is a form of the name *Judah*, a very popular Hebrew name. Judah was the chosen son of Jacob. It was from the tribe of Judah that our Savior came. He is *"the Lion of the tribe of Judah."*

There was a son named Judas or Jude in this family. He was born to Mary and Joseph after the virgin birth of Jesus Christ. Jude was the half brother of the Lord Jesus, having the same mother as Christ. He grew up in the same home in Nazareth. There are others in the Bible with this name, but this son of Mary and Joseph we believe to be the human author of the epistle of Jude.

Again in the Gospel according to Mark chapter six, verses one and two,

> *And he went out from thence, and came into his own country; and his disciples follow him. And when the sabbath day was come, he began to teach in the synagogue: and many hearing him were astonished, saying, From whence hath this man these things? and what wisdom is this which is given unto him, that even such mighty works are wrought by his hands?*

As Christ spoke, people from the Nazareth area identified Him with Mary and Joseph and their family members. They said, "What is so different about Him? There is something marvelously different." They were right. He was the virgin-born Son of God. He is the One who became man without ceasing to be God. He was God incarnate, robed in flesh. They could not explain it.

Then the people said in verse three, *"Is not this the carpenter, the son of Mary, the brother of James, and Joses, and of Juda, and Simon? and are not his sisters here with us? And they were offended at him."*

The Lord Jesus had more than one sister. The brothers are named here. Among this list of brothers is the name *Juda*. The son of Mary and Joseph, the same Jude who grew up in the home of Jesus Christ, was, we believe, the human instrument God used to pen this book of Jude.

Jude calls himself the servant of Jesus Christ. He opens this epistle with his heavenly relationship to Jesus Christ.

One could be a servant in New Testament times by being taken captive in battle or by being born into servanthood. The word used here in the first verse has to do with being born a servant, a bond slave.

He does not say, *"Jude, the servant of Jesus,"* speaking of the humanity of Christ. He says, *"Jude, the servant of Jesus Christ,"* speaking of the God-Man, the Anointed One. This is the truth for every Christian. We are born into God's family by faith in His Son. We are to serve our Lord. Have you been born into God's family? Are you a servant of Jesus Christ?

THE BOND OF THIS SERVANT

A bond slave or servant had a bond, something he was bound to do. That bond was very simple. The servant would always do the work of his master. Nothing would ever come before the master. Jude identifies his Master as the Lord Jesus Christ.

In this age of apostasy, we need to determine that our business in this world is not to see who we can master or what we can master but whom we are going to allow to master us. We need a master. I am glad that my Master is Jesus Christ.

In the marvelous wisdom of Almighty God, He has designed the Christian life so that when we give Him preeminence, things work best in our lives. Is Jesus Christ truly the One and only in our lives? Does He have the preeminence?

In the privacy of our home, there are times when my wife says things to me or puts her arm around me, letting me know by what she is doing that I am very special to her.

Recently while walking into the church, she put her hand on mine and said, "I love you and I am praying for you." It was not something she did for me that touched my heart. It was her love for me that touched my heart.

Do not confuse the matter of Christian service and Christian living. It is not first what we *do* for Him, but loving Him that our Lord wants. The bond of the servant is that his master is always preeminent.

Jude says, "I am a bond slave of Jesus Christ," using the word for servant that means "born into servanthood." Can you imagine growing up in the same household and saying, "I am born His servant"? This is what Jude said of the Lord Jesus Christ. His bond was that the Lord Jesus was always preeminent.

The Burden of This Servant

I use the word *burden* not to imply that what we do for Christ is unpleasant, because the Bible says that His commandments are not grievous. On the other hand, the Bible says, *"The way of transgressors is hard."* It is because God loves us that He makes the way of the transgressor hard. If He did not make the way of the transgressor hard, people would live in transgression continually. Every time it gets hard on the transgressor, the transgressor is caused to think, "The Lord's way is the best way."

What is our burden or our consuming passion as servants of the Lord Jesus? It is to love Him and serve Him from that heart of love. Who will do the work of the Lord? The servants of the Lord must do the work of the Lord.

As we walk through this hallway into the Revelation of Jesus Christ, notice carefully on the walls that there are examples of apostasy surrounding our walk. Our Lord desires to have servants who know that they have been born into His family and have a bond with Christ to do His work with their lives.

I am on this earth to do His work. There is no doubt in my mind, as I consider my life, that I am here to do His work. We must tell people how to be saved. If families are going to hear the truth, we must tell them the truth.

Recently, in a department store, I saw a lady with a little boy by her side. She was dragging him around and hitting at him as she dragged him. I saw her again in another place doing the same thing. I thought, "That woman needs someone to instruct her." One could be very critical of someone like that, but more than likely she has grown up without God and without God's Word and knows very little about the kind of discipline taught in the Word of God.

How are people going to know what God wants them to know? Someone who knows the truth must tell them the truth. We are His servants. We have been given His work to do. This is our job. God has raised up churches to do His work.

The Bible says in Revelation 1:1, *"The Revelation of Jesus Christ, which God gave unto him, to shew unto his servants things which must shortly come to pass."*

Notice that John uses the word *"servants."* Did you know that those of us who are saved, who are bond slaves of Jesus Christ, who have recognized our place in the family of God, have an awareness about the world that the world does not have about itself? We have an awareness about what is going on in the world, and we have an understanding that the world does not have.

We get this understanding from God. We know that there is a real heaven and a real hell. We know that there is a real Tribulation period and a real Antichrist coming. We know that there is a Great White Throne Judgment and a real lake of fire awaiting the lost. God has told us these things in His Word, and we believe Him.

> *The time is so short. The need is so great. The laborers are so few.*

Because of these things He has shown us, we are accountable to God to tell people the truth. We are the people who know the truth, have heard the truth, and have received the truth. As God's children, we must have a burden to get it out. So many are still in darkness. They are under the influence of the doctrines of demons. They are dying in the night of sin. We must get the message out! This is our responsibility in this age of apostasy. It is what God has given us to do.

A few years ago, a man on the staff of our church said, "I want to know what you want me to do. I want to understand your burden. I want to do what is necessary to understand the burden in your heart. I want to be a help to you." He came back a little later and said, "I've talked to your son. He has his father's heart. As I talked to your son, I realized that he is close enough to you and to your passion that he understands what you want."

I want to know what God wants done in the world He created. I want to know so that I can do it, not just to be informed. The better I get acquainted with His Son, the Lord Jesus, the more I know about the heart of God. Jesus Christ is God.

The time is so short. The need is so great. The laborers are so few. May the Spirit of God help us to be obedient to Christ as we study and apply these Bible lessons.

"Jude, the servant of Jesus Christ, and brother of James, to them that are sanctified by God the Father, and preserved in Jesus Christ, and called."

Jude 1

CHAPTER ONE

SANCTIFIED BY GOD THE FATHER

omething out of the ordinary is taking place in our world. It seems as though the Devil is getting in his last punches before the coming of our Savior. However, we should not be discouraged or downhearted. God is able, and where sin abounds, grace does much more abound. Greater is He that is in us than he that is in the world. We are on the victory side.

We are living in an age of apostasy. An *apostate* is one who has never trusted Christ as personal Savior but has looked at revealed truth and turned from it. It is impossible for a Christian to become an apostate because he is safe in the arms of the Lord Jesus, and as God's child he has *"eternal life."* We do not save ourselves, and we do not keep ourselves saved. According to what the Bible teaches, we are saved and kept by the grace of God.

The Bible says, *"Jude the servant of Jesus Christ, and brother of James."*

In our introduction, we found that Jude, the servant or bondslave of Jesus Christ, grew up in the home of the Lord Jesus. He was born to Mary and Joseph after the virgin birth of

Christ, but he does not refer to himself as a half brother of the Lord Jesus or as a child of Mary and Joseph. He makes no mention of his human relationship to the Lord Jesus. He says, *"Jude, the servant of Jesus Christ."* There are two ways to use the word *slave* or *bondslave*. One means "purchased or taken in battle." The other means "from birth." The term used here refers to a bondslave from birth.

This letter is written to those who know the Lord Jesus Christ as their personal Savior. Jude writes *"to them that are sanctified,"* but what does this truly mean? Before we take a closer look at this word, let us consider what the Bible says in I Peter 1:13-16,

> *Wherefore gird up the loins of your mind, be sober, and hope to the end for the grace that is to be brought unto you at the revelation of Jesus Christ; as obedient children, not fashioning yourselves according to the former lusts in your ignorance: but as he which hath called you is holy, so be ye holy in all manner of conversation; because it is written, Be ye holy; for I am holy.*

We are to live a holy life. The Bible continues in I Peter 1:17-19,

> *And if ye call on the Father, who without respect of persons judgeth according to every man's work, pass the time of your sojourning here in fear: forasmuch as ye know that ye were not redeemed with corruptible things, as silver and gold, from your vain conversation received by tradition from your fathers; but with the precious blood of Christ, as of a lamb without blemish and without spot.*

We have been purchased by the precious blood of Jesus Christ. For what purpose did God purchase us?

Occasionally, we take trips to the shopping mall, but when we go, impulsive buying can lead us to walk out of the mall with things that we did not intend to buy or with things that have no purpose. There should be a purpose for purchasing something. The Bible teaches that we have been redeemed by the precious blood of Jesus Christ for a special purpose.

Do you know that you are a Christian? Have you asked God to forgive your sin and by faith received Jesus Christ as your Savior? If so, the Bible says that you have been redeemed or purchased by the precious blood of Christ; you have been bought by His blood. Why have you been bought? You have been bought to be sanctified.

The Bible says in Hebrews 12:1-2,

> *Wherefore seeing we also are compassed about with so great a cloud of witnesses, let us lay aside every weight, and the sin which doth so easily beset us, and let us run with patience the race that is set before us, looking unto Jesus the author and finisher of our faith; who for the joy that was set before him endured the cross, despising the shame, and is set down at the right hand of the throne of God.*

Did you ever work hard to be able to purchase something? The labor may have been very difficult, but the purchase was sweet because of what you could do with it after the purchase. The Bible says that Jesus Christ endured the cross *"for the joy that was set before him."* No work has ever been done to compare with the work that Jesus Christ did on the cross of

Calvary. The greatest work ever done on earth was the work of Christ bleeding and dying on the cross for us. He knew no sin. Consider the labor of His love! The wrath of God rolled on Christ at Calvary when He became sin for us. He suffered, bled, and died *"for the joy that was set before him."*

WE ARE SET APART FOR GOD

First, the word *"sanctified"* means "to be set apart." The Bible says we are *"sanctified by God the Father."* The Lord Jesus Christ has purchased us with His own blood, and what He has purchased, He has sanctified. He sets His purchase apart for Himself. As a Christian, I belong to the Lord. I have been set apart for His use.

Speaking of creation, the Lord says in Genesis 2:1-3,

> *Thus the heavens and the earth were finished, and all the host of them. And on the seventh day God ended his work which he had made; and he rested on the seventh day from all his work which he had made. And God blessed the seventh day, and sanctified it: because that in it he had rested from all his work which God created and made.*

God's rest was not a rest from weariness; it was a rest of completion. He established the principle of the Sabbath. The Bible uses the word *"sanctified."* He set a day apart to make that day different from all other days. This use of the word helps to illustrate what God does with His children.

As Christians, in a world of billions of people, we have been bought by the blood of the Lord Jesus and have been set apart for something different than the rest of the world. We have been *"sanctified"* for God's use, set apart for the Lord.

We are to yield ourselves to God. Yielding our members for anything else is sin because the Lord has redeemed us for Himself. His witness in this world is His people. His work in this world is to be done through His people. God makes Himself known in this world through His people. We are *"sanctified;"* we are set apart for the Lord.

WE ARE DECLARED HOLY

Second, the word *"sanctified"* means "to declare or regard as holy." There is an old illustration that is sometimes used in connection with the word *sanctification* about a man who worked in a bar. He trusted the Lord Jesus Christ as his Savior. When he became a Christian, he wanted to get away from his sinful lifestyle. The desire to live a holy life gives evidence of salvation.

> *The greatest work ever done on earth was the work of Christ bleeding and dying on the cross for us.*

When the Lord comes into our lives, He gives power to deliver us from things that are sinful. There are many things that bind people's lives, and they think they can never get away from them. When Jesus Christ saves us, He sets us free. He gives us the power for victory over those things that bind us.

When this bartender became a Christian, he no longer wanted his job at the bar. He went to the owner of the bar and said, "I'd like to purchase one of the bar tables." He refinished the table and used it in his home as a reminder of where God had brought him from and what the Lord had done for him.

This table was no longer used for liquor glasses and gambling. It was now used for an entirely different purpose. It served as a constant reminder of the work God had accomplished in his life.

When we become Christians, God sanctifies us. He sets us apart for His service, and He begins at that moment to regard us as holy. He sees us through the blood of Jesus Christ and regards us as holy.

If we ask God to forgive us and cleanse us, He will, but there are times when Satan will try to use false guilt to bring us again into bondage.

No matter how I regard myself, if I am a Christian, God regards me as holy. He does not see my sin. He sees that my sin is covered in the blood of Jesus Christ, and He regards me as holy.

Before I trusted Christ as Savior, I thought that God would put all the good I did on one side and all the bad on the other. If I ever got too far behind, I would do more good and catch up before I died. I was scared to think that I might get killed while I was doing something bad and go to hell. What a terrible way to live!

We can never do enough good to get to heaven. The only way we can get to heaven is by the grace of God, not by our own goodness. We have already proven that we are sinners. If we have committed only one sin, it is against an infinite God and there is an infinite payment. That infinite payment means that we would die and go to hell trying to pay for it forever and still never fully make the payment.

When we come to Christ for salvation, God changes our record. He counts our sin paid for and imputes the righteousness of Jesus Christ to our account. He sees us as He sees His own dear Son, and He regards us as holy.

WE ARE TO BE HOLY

Third, the word *"sanctified"* means "to be holy." An Old Testament example of this is found in the book of Joshua. Moses, the servant of the Lord, had passed off the scene. Joshua, chosen as the leader of the people of Israel before the death of Moses, was leading the people into the Promised Land, across the Jordan into Canaan. Canaan is not a type or picture of heaven; it is a picture of the abundant Christian life. Unlike the time the Israelites walked through the Red Sea on dry ground, when the priests stepped up to the Jordan, they had to actually place their feet into the water, then the water opened and the people could walk through.

The Bible says in Joshua 3:1-5,

> *And Joshua rose early in the morning; and they removed from Shittim, and came to Jordan, he and all the children of Israel, and lodged there before they passed over. And it came to pass after three days, that the officers went through the host; and they commanded the people, saying, When ye see the ark of the covenant of the LORD your God, and the priests the Levites bearing it, then ye shall remove from your place, and go after it. Yet there shall be a space between you and it, about two thousand cubits by measure: come not near unto it, that ye may know the way by which ye must go: for ye*

*have not passed this way heretofore. And Joshua
said unto the people, Sanctify yourselves: for to
morrow the LORD will do wonders among you.*

"Sanctify yourselves." What does this mean? It means to be holy. It means that not only are we declared holy, not only have we been set apart for the Lord, but that we are to be holy people.

How is this possible? Joshua said to these people, *"Sanctify yourselves."* There are some who ridicule the thought of living a holy life. They need to read the Bible. The Christian life is a holy life. The only way to exemplify Jesus Christ in this world is by living a holy life.

If you desire to know how Christians should live, ask those who are not Christians. They will tell you where a Christian should go and where he should not go. They will tell you what a Christian should put into his body and what he should not put into his body.

Let us determine to have Bible-based convictions, but let our convictions be bathed in compassion. My mother said often, "Find people where they are and lead them to where you want them to be. Don't become so disillusioned with where they are that you simply forget them." The Lord Jesus found me where I was, and He is leading me to where He wants me to be. He desires to make me holy.

In John 17 we find the high priestly prayer of our Lord Jesus Christ. The Bible says in John 17:16-17, *"They are not of the world, even as I am not of the world. Sanctify them through thy truth: thy word is truth."*

Here the Lord speaks of His own children. How are we sanctified? How are we made holy? The Bible says, *"Sanctify them through thy truth: thy word is truth."* It is impossible to live a holy life apart from the Bible. We cannot be spiritual without being scriptural.

The easiest sins to name are the ones we do not commit, but God has made a way for His people to live a holy life.

When the Spirit of God moved Jude to write, he wrote, *"To them that are sanctified."*

> *It is impossible to live a holy life apart from the Bible. We cannot be spiritual without being scriptural.*

Let us praise the Lord for His wonderful work of sanctification in our lives and seek to live the holy lives He has called us to live.

*"Mercy unto you,
and peace,
and love, be
multiplied."*

Jude 2

CHAPTER
TWO

MERCY

he human instrument God used to pen this little book of one chapter was most likely a child born to Mary and Joseph after the virgin birth of Jesus Christ. He does not refer to his relationship to Christ in human terms, but begins by saying, *"Jude, the servant of Jesus Christ."* The word *"servant"* here means one born into slavery; he is declaring that by a spiritual birth he was a slave to Jesus Christ—a bondslave. The only desire of Jude's life was to please and serve the Lord.

"Jude, the servant of Jesus Christ, and brother of James, to them that are sanctified by God the Father...." *"Sanctified"* means "to be declared holy, regarded as holy, and becoming on a daily basis more like the Lord Jesus Christ." *"...sanctified by God the Father, and preserved in Jesus Christ, and called."*

The Word of God declares in verse two, *"Mercy unto you, and peace, and love, be multiplied."*

Not only do we find this word *"mercy"* in verse two, but we also find the divine order. The Bible says, *"Mercy. . . and peace, and love."* Before we can have peace and know love, we must have God's mercy.

The Bible says in Romans 5:1, *"Therefore being justified by faith, we have peace with God through our Lord Jesus Christ."* The Bible speaks of *"peace with God"* and then speaks of the *"peace of God"* in Philippians chapter four. This peace with God is because of God's mercy. We have peace, but it is impossible to have peace unless we first know of God's mercy.

The Word of God teaches that we are to have love multiplied. The Bible declares in John 13:34-35, *"A new commandment I give unto you, that ye love one another; as I have loved you, that ye also love one another. By this shall all men know that ye are my disciples, if ye have love one to another."*

I have a love relationship with God and with others who know the Lord. The fellowship of believers is a fellowship of love.

If I am going to know peace with God and have the peace of God and learn to love and let love be multiplied among the brethren, this must all begin with mercy. If I said to you that we have the grace of God extended to us, I would mean that God has extended something to us that we do not deserve. In the simplest definition, *grace* means "God giving us what we do not deserve." We have not earned it, and we cannot earn it. We do not merit it, and we cannot merit it, but God gives it to us.

If we say that we have mercy, we are declaring that God has withheld from us what we *do* deserve by the way of punishment, condemnation, and wrath. Jude writes, *"Mercy unto you."*

God Gives Mercy for Perilous Times

We are living in perilous times. Often we are filled with feelings of nostalgia, having the idea that living in the yesteryear would be much better than living in the present. People like to retreat to the past in their thinking. If we are not careful, we will live in some kind of fantasy world, envying bygone days, other eras, and past times. In God's wisdom and providence, He has allowed us to live in these times.

The times in which we live are perilous times. These are not ordinary times. In these perilous times, there is a certain spirit of anarchy in the land. It has always existed, but not with the same intensity as in these perilous times.

This church age had a beginning. The church started with Christ and His disciples and was empowered at Pentecost. It also has an ending. It consummates at the coming of Christ for His own. When we read the Revelation of Jesus Christ and finish the second and third chapters, we come to chapter four and realize the church can no longer be found. There is a great open door in heaven. The church is gone.

There is an ending, a concluding, of this age. Many believe that we are living in the end times of this age. Though we may refer to perilous times as any time during the church age, there is such a thing as the last of the last days.

God's Word says in II Timothy 3:1, *"This know also, that in the last days perilous times shall come."* Following this statement, the Lord gives us a list. The things on that list have always existed. They did not start in these perilous last days, but God calls our attention to the intensity of these things in our day.

The Bible says in verses two through four of II Timothy chapter three,

> *For men shall be lovers of their own selves, covetous, boasters, proud, blasphemers, disobedient to parents, unthankful, unholy, without natural affection, trucebreakers, false accusers, incontinent, fierce, despisers of those that are good. Traitors, heady, highminded, lovers of pleasures more than lovers of God.*

Notice what the Bible says in verse five, *"Having a form of godliness, but denying the power thereof: from such turn away."*

The most dangerous thing in these perilous times is not what we find in verses two through four, but what we find in verse five, *"having a form of godliness."*

What makes these last days so perilous, so risky, and so dangerous is apostasy, meaning "religion without truth." This is the distinguishing characteristic of these last days. The earth is filled with religion. We have religion everywhere, but it is religion without the true God, without Christ, and without the Bible.

The Bible says that the church is the pillar and the ground of the truth. God has deposited the truth in the church by His Word and His Spirit. We are to communicate the truth of God in every age and in every generation. The church is to lift up the truth in love.

The Bible is the Book of truth. No wonder there is such an attack on the Bible. Every word of the Bible is the Word of God. It is without error.

There is a great need for those who know God to take a compassionate stand for the truth. We are living in perilous times. What makes these times so perilous is this form of godliness, this religion without God's Word, without truth, and without Christ. We have been called of God to live at this time. In these perilous times, God says, *"Mercy unto you."*

ALL PEOPLE NEED MERCY

We deserve justice but need mercy. This should help some of us who are so self-righteous in our judgment of others. All people need mercy.

At times in our lives, we come to the place when we feel as if we deserve mercy. We need mercy, but we do not deserve mercy. God has a way of showing us our helplessness and our sinfulness. What we really deserve, because of our sin, is the wrath of God.

In these perilous times, people need mercy. The Bible says in John 3:36, *"He that believeth on the Son hath everlasting life: and he that believeth not the Son shall not see life; but the wrath of God abideth on him."*

The Bible says, *"The wrath of God abideth on him."* This means that everyone who does not know Jesus Christ has the wrath of God already abiding on him. We have in our minds that someday people are going to have the wrath of God on them. Not someday, but this day, all people without the Lord Jesus have the wrath of God abiding on them.

Salvation is not educating one's self into heaven. Salvation is an act of God's grace and mercy. It is instantaneous. A man is saved the moment he trusts Jesus Christ for forgiveness of his sin. It is a work of God. It is a miraculous work. We are under the wrath of God, and we need mercy. When we pray for salvation, we say, "Lord, forgive my sin. I don't want to die and go to hell. Lord Jesus, hear my prayer. Be merciful to me." By His mercy, He forgives our sin and saves us.

> *What makes these last days so perilous, so risky, and so dangerous is apostasy, meaning "religion without truth."*

The lost world, because of the darkness in which they live, may occasionally look at some of us and say, "You think you are better than we are." This is not what we think. We live the Christian life because God has saved us, and we do not want to go back to the things of the past because of His mercy toward us.

Because people need mercy, God says, "Mercy unto you."

WE SHOULD PRAY FOR MERCY

The Word of God says, *"Mercy unto you,"* but we must pray for mercy.

Habakkuk was an Old Testament prophet living in the southern kingdom of Judah. The northern kingdom had already gone into Assyrian captivity, and the southern kingdom of Judah was on the threshold of being taken captive. They were about to be overtaken by Babylon, led by Nebuchadnezzar the Great. Judah would fall to Babylon and be carried away into captivity.

Habakkuk was called by God to serve on the eve of the captivity of the nation of Judah. He already knew there was a serious problem in Judah. He approached God saying, "There is sin in the land, and, Lord, I don't know why something is not done about it." Then God said to him, "I'm going to do something about it. I am going to send the Babylonians down to judge Judah and to destroy the land and carry the people away into captivity." Habakkuk said, "Lord, that is too heavy a judgment." God said to Habakkuk, "It is going to happen."

In other words, the inevitable judgment of God is going to come. This has helped me as much as anything else I have ever found in the Word of God. There is something here that cannot be changed. There are things that have happened in people's lives that cannot be undone. No matter how sympathetic you get over it, certain things cannot be undone. Yet, we have victory through faith.

We have forgiveness because of the mercy of God. When there is repentance of sin, there can be forgiveness and restoration, but there are things that happen to people that cannot be changed.

> *The Bible is the Book of truth. No wonder there is such an attack on the Bible.*

Our nation is on a collision course. Years ago I heard old preachers say, "If God doesn't judge America, He will have to apologize to Sodom and Gomorrah." The truth of the matter is that God is not going to apologize to anyone because He always does right.

We are a nation blessed beyond other nations on the earth. I love America and thank God to be an American, but we may wake up in the morning and hear that something catastrophic has happened in our own nation. We may hear of a national collapse in the next few weeks or months. What we need to pray for in the midst of wrath is mercy.

Habakkuk said in chapter three, "All right, Lord. You are going to judge our nation. I cannot hold back the judgment, but here is what I am praying." The Bible says in Habakkuk 3:1-2,

> *A prayer of Habakkuk the prophet upon Shigionoth. O LORD, I have heard thy speech, and was afraid: O LORD, revive thy work in the midst of the years, in the midst of the years make known; in wrath remember mercy.*

He prayed for mercy. Seek God every day for mercy. Each of us should pray, "God, be merciful to our nation. God, be merciful to my family. God, be merciful to our church. God, be merciful to me." Our prayer for the mercy of God is evidence of a right attitude toward the holiness of the Lord and the sinfulness of man.

In these perilous times, we must recognize our need of mercy and pray that God would extend His mercy to us as individuals and as a nation.

"Beloved, when I gave all diligence to write unto you of the common salvation, it was needful for me to write unto you, and exhort you that ye should earnestly contend for the faith which was once delivered unto the saints.

For there are certain men crept in unawares, who were before of old ordained to this condemnation, ungodly men, turning the grace of our God into lasciviousness, and denying the only Lord God, and our Lord Jesus Christ."

Jude 3-4

CHAPTER THREE

EARNESTLY CONTEND
FOR THE FAITH

ur faith was *"once delivered,"* but it must be contended for in each generation. This Bible passage says, *"It was needful."* Contending for the faith is not simply a good idea; it is an absolute necessity.

The Bible says in Acts 17:1-3,

Now when they had passed through Amphipolis and Apollonia, they came to Thessalonica, where was a synagogue of the Jews: and Paul, as his manner was, went in unto them, and three sabbath days reasoned with them out of the scriptures, opening and alleging, that Christ must needs have suffered, and risen again from the dead; and that this Jesus, whom I preach unto you, is Christ.

Notice this expression, *"must needs."* There is no way our salvation could have been accomplished without the cross. *"Christ must needs have suffered."* When Jude, under the inspiration of the Spirit of God, penned the words in the epistle of Jude, God declared to us that there was something that was *"needful."* It *"must needs"* be done.

In education, there are courses we call electives; they are not required to be taken. There are other courses that are requirements. In order to finish a course of study, the required courses must be completed.

The Lord says, "What I am writing to you in this passage is not an elective; it is a requirement. It is needful."

Notice again verse three of Jude, *"Beloved, when I gave all diligence to write unto you of the common salvation."* He is not saying here in this verse, "I was going to write to you about one thing, but my mind was changed." He says, "I was led of the Spirit of God to write this and to take this particular path concerning our common salvation." He is saying that it is impossible to speak of our *"common salvation"* unless we are willing to contend for the faith.

> *Our faith was "once delivered," but it must be contended for in each generation.*

The word *"beloved"* means "loved of God." How wonderful it is to know that there is nothing we can do to make God love us less or make God love us more! We are His beloved. We are loved of God.

The word *"exhort"* means "to plead or persuade." *"Contend"* means "to stand agonizingly, seriously." *"The faith"* is the body of doctrine we believe.

Though there was a particular audience to whom this letter was first read, we understand that this verse is to all believers. It is not only for all time; it is to all believers for all time. This verse is not limited to preachers or what we might refer to as "full-time Christian servants." It is directed to all God's children for all time.

> *It is impossible to speak of our* "common salvation" *unless we are willing to contend for the faith.*

In other words, God says that every Christian should earnestly contend for the faith. If you are a Christian, it is just as important for you to earnestly contend for the faith as it is for the pastor of your church to earnestly contend for the faith. If you are one of the beloved, it is your responsibility to contend for the faith. It is needful that we contend for the faith. Remember, there can be no message of the *"common salvation"* unless we contend for the faith.

We contend for the faith when we stand for what we find in the Word of God. We contend for the faith when we strengthen and hold up the hands of those who are teaching and preaching God's Word. We contend for the faith when we encourage the pastor. We contend for the faith when we give out gospel literature. We contend for the faith when we stand in a Sunday School class and teach the truth to others. We contend for the faith when we resist error and call it by name. We contend for the faith when we proclaim the gospel message.

Every Christian needs to be a contender for the faith. This means it is our business to get agonizingly serious about contending for the faith. There is someone in this world who will never see any other Christian except you. That person will never know anything about Jesus Christ except what he knows about Him from your life.

The faith that we are called to contend for in the book of Jude is our body of doctrine. The Bible says in I Corinthians 15:1-3, *"Moreover, brethren, I declare unto you the gospel which I preached unto you, which also ye have received, and wherein ye stand."* We are contending for *salvation*, the message of the gospel.

The Bible continues, *"By which also ye are saved, if ye keep in memory what I preached unto you, unless ye have believed in vain. For I delivered unto you first of all that which I also received, how that Christ died for our sins according to the scriptures."* We are contending for the *substitutionary death* of the Lord Jesus Christ for our sin. We are also contending for the *Scriptures*. We believe in the verbal, plenary inspiration of Scripture. Every word in the Bible is the Word of God. All of it is the Word of God, and it is without error. God has preserved His Word, and we hold it in our hands and should hide it in our hearts. The Bible continues in I Corinthians 15:4, *"And that he was buried, and that he rose again the third day according to the scriptures."*

> *If you are a Christian, it is just as important for you to earnestly contend for the faith as it is for the pastor of your church to earnestly contend for the faith.*

We are contending for the *bodily resurrection* of the Lord Jesus Christ. He came forth bodily from the dead, alive forevermore.

The Bible makes a very powerful statement to us in Revelation chapter three. As God addressed the church in Sardis, He said in verse one,

> *And unto the angel of the church in Sardis write; these things saith he that hath the seven Spirits of God, and the seven stars; I know thy works, that thou hast a name that thou livest, and art dead.*

The Lord Jesus had a specific message for each of these churches, and He addressed them by referring to Himself with a specific title. As He spoke to each of the seven churches, each message was different.

The very next words in verse two are, *"Be watchful, and strengthen the things which remain."* Professing Christians are drifting in record numbers. What remains must be strengthened. How do we strengthen the things which remain? We strengthen them by contending, by standing seriously, by agonizingly taking a stand for God, by proclaiming the truth and crying out against error.

Remember, our faith was once delivered, but it must be contended for in each generation.

CONTEND WITH CONVICTIONS

If we are going to contend, we must contend with convictions. Our convictions come from God's Word. They are Bible-based.

Under the inspiration of the Spirit of God, Jude penned in verse three,

> *Beloved, when I gave all diligence to write unto you of the common salvation, it was needful*

*for me to write unto you, and exhort you that ye
should earnestly contend for the faith which was
once delivered unto the saints.*

Our faith was once delivered. We do not need another delivery
of the faith; we do not need a new faith. We need to contend for
the faith that was once delivered. We must not change what is
proven and tested and has been authoritatively given to us based
on the Word of God. We simply need to preach the same truth that
has been preached to people for all ages.

We owe a great debt to those who have taken a stand for the truth,
to those who have contended for the faith so that we could know it.
We may get by without contending, but if we do not contend, there
will be nothing left to contend for in the next generation.

The Bible says in Galatians 1:6-8,

*I marvel that ye are so soon removed from him
that called you into the grace of Christ unto
another gospel: which is not another; but there
be some that trouble you, and would pervert the
gospel of Christ. But though we, or an angel
from heaven, preach any other gospel unto you
than that which we have preached unto you, let
him be accursed.*

Paul said that if a man preaches something other than the
truth of God, let him be accursed.

He continues in verse nine, *"As we said before, so say I now
again, If any man preach any other gospel unto you than that ye
have received, let him be accursed."*

Notice that he said, *"Than that ye have received."* How do we pass this along from one generation to the next? We receive it from faithful followers of the Lord, and we faithfully give it to others.

Paul wrote the church in Corinth in II Corinthians 4:8-13,

> *We are troubled on every side, yet not distressed; we are perplexed, but not in despair; persecuted, but not forsaken; cast down, but not destroyed; always bearing about in the body the dying of the Lord Jesus, that the life also of Jesus might be made manifest in our body. For we which live are alway delivered unto death for Jesus' sake, that the life also of Jesus might be made manifest in our mortal flesh. So then death worketh in us, but life in you. We having the same spirit of faith, according as it is written, I believed, and therefore have I spoken; we also believe, and therefore speak.*

We do not need another delivery of the faith; we do not need a new faith. We need to contend for the faith that was once delivered.

He quoted Psalm 116:10, *"I believed, therefore have I spoken: I was greatly afflicted."* Why do we say what we say? Because we believe what we believe. We believe what we believe because we get it from the Word of God, and we speak it because we believe it. We must contend with convictions–Bible-based, sin-hating, Holy Spirit-empowered, and Christ-honoring convictions.

Contend With Compassion

We must contend with compassion. Be thankful for convictions. If we must choose between position and disposition, we should choose the right position and the wrong disposition rather than the right disposition and the wrong position; but conviction without compassion is not Christlike. Our compassion should run as deep as our convictions run high.

Pastors should preach the truth without fear of man. They should lift up the truth in love. The preacher must be unafraid to preach the truth. People who love God will love the preacher who preaches the truth.

If the preacher does not step on your toes every once in a while, there is something wrong with his preaching. It is a shame that many people can come to church and never be moved or stirred and can leave the same way they came. The pastor can say whatever needs to be said as long as the people know that he loves them. May we live the kind of lives that are devoted to Christ and given in service to others so that people know that we genuinely love them.

As Christians, we are not down on sinners; we are down on sin. The Lord Jesus came to redeem lost sinners. It is the love of God that saved us. *"For God so loved the world...."* This must be our motive.

We must contend with conviction, but we need to contend with compassion. May these two things always be true of our lives and of our churches. May people say, "I hear the truth at that church, and I can tell that they truly love people."

Compassion is not something we work up that amounts to no more than a social charm for the well-being of others. Christian compassion comes from abiding in Christ.

CONTEND CONTINUALLY

We cannot contend in one generation and stop in the next generation because the generation where we stop contending is the one we lose. There is no place to stop. We must contend continually. We are to contend year after year. If we stop contending for a week, it will show up somewhere.

A well-conditioned athlete will tell you that he devotes so much time each day to practice. He will also tell you that if he does not pay the price each day, the spectators, the coach, and the competitors may not know it as quickly, but it will show up in his body.

There is no day to let up. The Devil is as a roaring lion. He walks by the cage of our lives. He will walk by a thousand times to find the door open one time. The day that we let up will be the day he walks by and finds the door open.

The book of Jude can be divided into two parts; the first part speaks of our *duty*. The Word of God says that we are to *"earnestly contend for the faith which was once delivered unto the saints."* The second part of the book speaks of our *danger*. Verse four says, *"For there are certain men crept in unawares."* The Holy Spirit declares that the reason for writing is to confront us with our duty to earnestly contend for the faith and to declare the danger that certain men have crept in unawares. We need to be awakened to our duty and to our danger.

If we are going to contend continually, there are dangers to be faced. The Bible says that certain people have crept in unawares to change things in the church. Why is it so important that we mark these creepers? The Bible says in I Timothy 3:15, *"But if I tarry long, that thou mayest know how thou oughtest to behave thyself in the house of God, which is the church of the living God, the pillar and ground of the truth."*

> *Conviction without compassion is not Christlike. Our compassion should run as deep as our convictions run high.*

The church has the God-given responsibility to declare the truth. The church of the living God is to influence a community, a city, a county, a state, and in some ways, a nation. A standard of holy living is raised by the people who fear God and follow His Word.

If people can creep in and change what others believe is true, what a damnable thing has been accomplished! No wonder Jude warns us of this danger!

Who are these creepers? Let us take note of what God's Word says about them.

THEY CREPT IN UNAWARES

This means that they took their place alongside other people who actually believed the truth without anyone realizing they were there. The Bible says in I John 2:18-19,

> *Little children, it is the last time: and as ye have heard that antichrist shall come, even now are there many antichrists; whereby we know that it is the last time. They went out from us, but*

*they were not of us; for if they had been of us,
they would no doubt have continued with us: but
they went out, that they might be made manifest
that they were not all of us.*

John, led by the Spirit of God, said that there was a time when certain people who were really not part of us were identified with us. He uses the expression *"antichrist."*

The word *"antichrist"* can be used to identify anyone or anything that is against or instead of Christ. Notice that these who were against Christ, instead of Christ, these profaners of Christ, were once numbered with Christian people. They got inside. They *"crept in unawares."*

Across America and around the world, there are churches calling themselves Christian that are filled with these kinds of people. They do not believe the Bible. They do not believe the Lord Jesus Christ. Slowly, there has been a change in these so-called Christian places. These people came in unawares.

THEIR CONDEMNATION WAS FORETOLD

Jude 4 says, *"For there are certain men crept in unawares, who were before of old ordained to this condemnation."*

This means that their condemnation was foretold. God said that these kinds of people would exist. Many main-line denominational groups, many churches that once stood for truth, and many groups and organizations where great-grandfathers and great-grandmothers heard the truth and are now identified with the same movement, are really no longer Bible-believing movements. They have changed. Christ is no longer honored.

53

This is one of the reasons I am glad to be an independent Baptist. The New Testament pattern for a local church proves to be autonomous, self-governing, and a part of no denominational hierarchy. We are under Christ and following the Lord. Our loyalty must be to Jesus Christ and to Him alone. The sole authority for our faith and practice is the Bible. Our leadership comes from the Holy Spirit of God.

Some good people you may know and love are caught up in something they have been in for years that has left its original moorings and no longer believes what the Word of God teaches. They may even say that we are intolerant because we do not make some sort of religious umbrella and bring everyone underneath it. But they would not say you were intolerant for refusing a drop of poison to be placed in a drink. They would not say you were intolerant for refusing to allow a poisonous snake in a baby's playpen. May the Lord help us to stand! The soul of man is eternal. The eternal destiny of people is at stake.

It is not our responsibility to make the message acceptable; it is our responsibility to make the message available, to speak the truth and lift up Jesus Christ, and to proclaim God's Word. We should stand where the Bible has always stood. We are not to be moved from it.

Their condemnation was foretold. The Bible says in II Peter 2:1-3,

> *But there were false prophets also among the people, even as there shall be false teachers among you, who privily shall bring in damnable heresies, even denying the Lord that bought them and bring upon themselves swift destruction. And many shall follow their pernicious ways; by reason of whom the way of truth shall be evil spoken of. And through*

covetousness shall they with feigned words make merchandise of you: whose judgment now of a long time lingereth not, and their damnation slumbereth not.

We have been warned about these people. If we are going to contend continually, we will certainly encounter men who desire to destroy and deny the things that we know to be true from God's Word.

THEIR CONDUCT SHOULD BE MARKED

We are to love people and to do good to all men, especially, the Bible says, to them who are of the household of faith. But the Bible also says that there are certain people who should be marked.

God's Word says in Jude 4, *"For there are certain men crept in unawares."* He says, *"certain men,"* as if he knows who they are. Their conduct should be marked.

The Bible says in Romans 16:17, *"Now I beseech you, brethren, mark them which cause divisions and offences contrary to the doctrine which ye have learned; and avoid them."*

We must mark them and avoid them. This may not sound very loving, but it is being very protective of the pillar and ground of the truth. By doing this, we keep things right.

Their conduct should be marked. Speaking of their conduct, the Bible says that they are *"ungodly."* This word means *"refusing to submit to God."* They are ungodly because they refuse to submit to the Lord. Our Lord desires that we yield our lives to Him.

Notice also about their conduct that they turn the grace of God into *"lasciviousness."* This word means "unleashing desire." Almost every time this word is used, it has to do with sexual behavior. It means "doing whatever one feels like doing." Some people may use the grace of God to say, "We're free." Yes, we are free, but the Christian is free to do what the Lord Jesus desires for him to do. The beautiful thing about the Christian life is that, as we yield to God, we desire to do the right thing with our lives.

Notice the third thing concerning their conduct. The Bible says in Jude 4, *"And denying the only Lord God...."* This expression has to do with our sovereign God, the God of the universe. *"...and our Lord Jesus Christ."* He is speaking of the God of the saved, our Lord, our Savior, Jesus Christ, the promised Messiah. They deny the Lord Jesus Christ. These came in unawares and finally wound up denying the Lord Jesus.

> *People who love God will love the preacher who preaches the truth.*

As we resolve to contend continually, we must remember that these men who creep in unawares, whose condemnation was foretold, whose conduct must be marked, are dangers that we must face. If we face these dangers trusting in Christ, we will become stronger in Him.

I thought when God called me to the ministry that I could establish what I believed and then live off that for the rest of my life. I have found that our faith and trust in the Lord must be renewed every day and that I am called upon to take a stronger stand today because of the increasing wickedness in the world.

When the Bible says, *"It was needful for me to write unto you, and exhort you that ye should earnestly contend for the faith,"* that is exactly what God meant. Let us not be ashamed to contend with convictions, with compassion, and to do it continually.

"I will therefore put you in remembrance, though ye once knew this, how that the Lord, having saved the people out of the land of Egypt, afterward destroyed them that believed not. And the angels which kept not their first estate, but left their own habitation, he hath reserved in everlasting chains under darkness unto the judgment of the great day. Even as Sodom and Gomorrha, and the cities about them in like manner, giving themselves over to fornication, and going after strange flesh, are set forth for an example, suffering the vengeance of eternal fire."

Jude 5-7

SET FORTH FOR
AN EXAMPLE

here are two great teaching methods given in this passage. The first one is found in verse five, *"I will therefore put you in remembrance."* The teacher is to use repetition. The second one is found in verse seven, *"Set forth for an example."* It is teaching by example. *Repetition* and *by example* are two great teaching methods. God repeats things, and we should not be afraid to repeat things that need to be repeated.

Allow me to reinforce this with a verse of Scripture from the Old Testament. The Bible says in Isaiah 28:10, *"For precept must be upon precept, precept upon precept; line upon line, line upon line; here a little, and there a little."*

One entire book of the Bible is given to us as a second account–the book of Deuteronomy. Many times God says again and again the same thing, yet not one word in the Bible is redundant. People sometimes say, "I've heard that before." Rejoice–it bears repeating!

In Jude 7, the Lord concludes this passage by saying that these things are given to us for an example. The Bible says in I Corinthians 10:1-12,

> *Moreover, brethren, I would not that ye should be ignorant, how that all our fathers were under the cloud, and all passed through the sea; and were all baptized unto Moses in the cloud and in the sea; and did all eat the same spiritual meat; and did all drink the same spiritual drink; for they drank of that spiritual Rock that followed them: and that Rock was Christ. But with many of them God was not well pleased: for they were overthrown in the wilderness. Now these things were our examples, to the intent we should not lust after evil things, as they also lusted. Neither be ye idolaters, as were some of them; as it is written, The people sat down to eat and drink, and rose up to play. Neither let us commit fornication, as some of them committed, and fell in one day three and twenty thousand. Neither let us tempt Christ, as some of them also tempted, and were destroyed of serpents. Neither murmur ye, as some of them also murmured, and were destroyed of the destroyer. Now all these things happened unto them for ensamples: and they are written for our admonition, upon whom the ends of the world are come. Wherefore let him that thinketh he standeth take heed lest he fall.*

God said, *"Now all these things happened unto them for ensamples: and they are written for our admonition."* When we come to the book of Jude, the Lord concludes the seventh verse by saying, *"Set forth for an example, suffering the vengeance of eternal fire."*

God declares to us that these apostates will be judged. He gives us examples of judgment, saying to us, "If you doubt that God is a God of judgment, then remember these examples. If you doubt that the apostates will be judged, then remember these examples."

The Bible says in Galatians 6:7, *"For whatsoever a man soweth, that shall he also reap."* God says, "Here are some examples." We need to learn from these examples.

One of the reasons many have drifted so far from God is that they have failed to heed these examples. Some examples are good examples of things that should be emulated in our lives. Some are bad examples, but they serve a great purpose—to show us what not to do.

THE EXAMPLE OF ISRAEL

God's Word says in Jude 5, *"I will therefore put you in remembrance, though ye once knew this, how that the Lord, having saved the people out of the land of Egypt, afterward destroyed them that believed not."*

The word *"saved"* used in this verse is used for a physical deliverance. A mixed multitude came out of Egypt, but collectively Jude is referring to God's people. The Bible says that after the Lord delivered them, He destroyed those who did not believe.

God recalls this example for us in the book of Numbers. In the fourteenth chapter of the book of Numbers, the spies were sent out. There were twelve of them, one from each of the twelve tribes of the nation of Israel. They spied out the land of Canaan. They were out forty days and came back with an evil report. Yes, the land was a land of milk and honey. They brought back grapes in a cluster so great that one man could not carry them. But they told the people that there were giants in the land. Ten of the spies said, "We are like grasshoppers in their sight." They would not believe God and began to murmur and complain.

The Bible says in Numbers 14:1-2,

> *And all the congregation lifted up their voice, and cried; and the people wept that night. And all the children of Israel murmured against Moses and against Aaron: and the whole congregation said unto them, Would God that we had died in the land of Egypt!*

Did God hear them? He not only heard them say this, He later reminded them that He had heard what they said. Remember this solemn warning: Be careful what you say because God is listening. God Almighty heard the children of Israel murmuring and complaining. And, just as the Bible promises, they reaped what they had sown. They spoke of putting to death their leaders and going back to Egypt. The Bible says in Number 14:28-34,

> *Say unto them, As truly as I live, saith the Lord, as ye have spoken in mine ears, so will I do to you: your carcases shall fall in this wilderness; and all that were numbered of you, according to your whole number, from twenty years old and upward, which have murmured against me, doubtless ye shall not come into the land, concerning which I sware to make you dwell therein, save Caleb the son of Jephunneh, and Joshua the son of Nun. But your little ones,*

which ye said should be a prey, them will I bring in, and they shall know the land which ye have despised. But as for you, your carcases, they shall fall in this wilderness. And your children shall wander in the wilderness forty years, and bear your whoredoms, until your carcases be wasted in the wilderness. After the number of the days in which ye searched the land, even forty days, each day for a year, shall ye bear your iniquities, even forty years, and ye shall know my breach of promise.

God dealt with His own people, the children of Israel. These people were the ones He redeemed from bondage. They put the blood on the lentil and the side posts, and the death angel passed over. God opened up the Red Sea and brought them through on dry ground. Yet, He judged His own people. If God judged them, He will certainly judge others as well.

It is a serious thing when a person who has been blessed by God does not behave like someone who has been blessed by God. For forty years the children of Israel felt the hand of God's judgment until physical death came. After the frustration of wandering in the wilderness, death must have come as a relief. No doubt, many were dying all the time. Think of how many years many of them had to bear the sentence of death and then die. God hears what we say, and He deals with His people. They suffered a physical death in the wilderness.

In I Corinthians chapter five, the apostle Paul addressed a case in the church at Corinth and said in verse one, *"It is reported commonly that there is fornication among you, and such fornication as is not so much as named among the Gentiles, that one should have his father's wife."*

He named the sin. I would to God that we had many more preachers who would name sin. It is not a pleasant thing to do. It is not a popular thing for people to hear, but more preachers need to name sin where they find it.

The Bible says in I Corinthians 5:2-5, *"And ye are puffed up, and have not rather mourned, that he that hath done this deed might be taken away from among you...."*

They should have been brokenhearted. They did not mourn about the sin, nor did they mourn about the judgment that was coming to this individual.

> *For I verily, as absent in body, but present in spirit, have judged already, as though I were present, concerning him that hath so done this deed, in the name of our Lord Jesus Christ, when ye are gathered together, and my spirit, with the power of our Lord Jesus Christ, to deliver such an one unto Satan for the destruction of the flesh, that the spirit may be saved in the day of the Lord Jesus.*

He said that it is possible to be delivered to the Devil for the destruction of the flesh. The Bible says in I John 5:16,

> *If any man see his brother sin a sin which is not unto death, he shall ask, and he shall give him life for them that sin not unto death. There is a sin unto death: I do not say that he shall pray for it.*

This message is to God's people. There is a sin unto death for saved people. The Bible clearly teaches that it is possible for a Christian to die prematurely. There are instances in Scripture like

I Corinthians 11:30-32 where the Lord teaches us that Christians who continued in sin were chastened with premature death.

God delivered His people and He judged them. For forty years, they died in the wilderness. If God judged His own people, be certain that He will judge these apostates as well.

THE EXAMPLE OF THE ANGELS

The first example is of those who came out of Egypt. The second example is in verse six and speaks of the angels *"which kept not their first estate."* The Bible says, *"And the angels which kept not their first estate, but left their own habitation, he hath reserved in everlasting chains under darkness unto the judgment of the great day."*

These were beautiful angels, angels who rebelled against God and were judged for their rebellion.

God says that they *"kept not their first estate, but left their own habitation."* We are told that these expressions have to do with their manner of life. The word *"habitation"* has to do with their dwelling as individual angels.

There is a record in Genesis six where the *"sons of God"* married the *"daughters of men,"* and they produced giants in the land. This was before the old world was destroyed by the flood. Many good men believe these *"sons of God"* were spirit beings. There are other good men who believe it is simply a record of the unsaved marrying the saved. When the line of Seth and the line of Cain came together, the line of separation was broken and the judgment of God came upon them.

Some believe that this particular verse in Jude, verse six, is a commentary on Genesis six and explains what happened to those *"sons of God."* Not all the fallen angels are reserved in judgment. Some of those angels are known as the demon spirits who move freely about in our world today. Others are bound and chained, reserved for judgment. There is great demonic activity in the world today. Some Bible teachers say that the ones who are bound are the ones that defiled the flesh and got involved with the human race in Genesis chapter six. What I do know is that God says that there were angels who left their own habitation.

> *There lurks inside every one of us a beast seeking to get into something evil.*

They left their own habitation, and they are reserved under darkness in chains until the judgment of the great day. God gives us another example. He speaks of the group of fallen angels who rebelled along with Satan. Perhaps a third of the angels rebelled with the Devil. The Bible says in Revelation 12:4,

> *And his tail drew the third part of the stars of heaven, and did cast them to the earth: and the dragon stood before the woman which was ready to be delivered, for to devour her child as soon as it was born.*

God judged these angels, these created beings, these ministering spirits. God judged them and He is going to cast them into the lake of fire.

What about someone who has done such mighty things, someone who has accomplished so much good? If God will judge angels, no one will escape. The truth is that God judged these angels that sinned, and He will surely judge the apostates.

THE EXAMPLE OF SODOM AND GOMORRAH

The third example is found in verse seven,

> *Even as Sodom and Gomorrha, and the cities about them in like manner, giving themselves over to fornication, and going after strange flesh, are set forth for an example, suffering the vengeance of eternal fire.*

In Jude 4, as the Lord begins to talk about the behavior of the apostates, He states first that they are ungodly, second, that they have turned the grace of God into lasciviousness, and third, that they have denied the only Lord God and our Lord Jesus Christ. He gives examples of each of these things in the following three verses.

When we come to the sin of Sodom and Gomorrah, turning the grace of God into lasciviousness, we know that these sinners, these fornicators in Sodom and Gomorrah, committed the awful sin of homosexuality. God gives this account as an example of judgment. The Bible says that they went after strange flesh. The word *"strange"* in this context means "that which did not belong to them."

There lurks inside every one of us a beast seeking to get into something evil. It is our old nature. Many people say that they just happened to fall into sin. This is not how we get into sin. We have an evil beast inside of us that searches for something sinful. The most degenerate behavior among human beings, according to Romans chapter one, is exemplified in homosexual behavior.

God says in Romans 1:26 that this is *"vile affection."* God uses the word *"vile."* It is not a lovely couple trying to do something socially beneficial for the rest of the world; it is *"vile affection."* God destroyed Sodom and Gomorrah for such sin.

The Bible says in Luke 10:10-11,

> *But into whatsoever city ye enter, and they receive you not, go your ways out into the streets of the same, and say, Even the very dust of your city, which cleaveth on us, we do wipe off against you: notwithstanding be ye sure of this, that the kingdom of God is come nigh unto you.*

Our Lord speaks here of going out witnessing and not being received. In this context, notice the twelfth verse. The Lord Jesus says, *"But I say unto you, that it shall be more tolerable in that day for Sodom, than for that city."*

Sodom never had the light we have.

Sodom, as a city, is mentioned twice as many times as Gomorrah, so evidently Sodom was the leading city in fornication and homosexuality. God takes the worst of the two cities and says, "The worst of the cities of the plains, Sodom, will be tolerated more in judgment than that city."

Here is the point. Sodom never had the light we have. We live in a county with churches on every corner and radio broadcasts going out daily about Jesus Christ. Tens of thousands of gospel tracts are distributed each day.

If we are going to preach about the judgment of God on Sodom and Gomorrah, we must realize what light we are presently sinning against. Let us awaken to our individual responsibility before God.

These examples are given to us to drive home the seriousness of apostasy. The Bible says in Hebrews 12:29, *"Our God is a consuming fire."* When dealing with the souls of men, we are dealing with an extremely serious matter. It is a matter of heaven or hell. Let us determine to take a clear, compassionate stand for the truth, realizing that, as we stand, we are going against the grain of accepted religious practices.

"Likewise also these filthy dreamers defile the flesh, despise dominion, and speak evil of dignities."

Jude 8

CHAPTER FIVE

THESE FILTHY DREAMERS

 ost everyone knows that something is tragically wrong in our world.

Many make strong declarations saying that they do not need God and certainly do not believe the Bible. Some of these same people speak of a return to values, but God's people know that without God's Word, there are no absolutes; there is no fixed point of reference from which to point to specific values.

The Bible says in Jude 8, *"Likewise also these filthy dreamers defile the flesh, despise dominion, and speak evil of dignities."*

These *"filthy dreamers"* are guilty of three distinct things. The intent of the expression *"filthy dreamers"* is to emphasize the fact that they have no pure thought.

God declares in His Word that *"these filthy dreamers defile the flesh, despise dominion, and speak evil of dignities."* When God says *"Likewise,"* He is making reference to what we find in verses five through seven,

I will therefore put you in remembrance, though ye once knew this, how that the Lord, having saved the people out of the land of Egypt, afterward destroyed them that believed not. And the angels which kept not their first estate, but left their own habitation, he hath reserved in everlasting chains under darkness unto the judgment of the great day. Even as Sodom and Gomorrha, and the cities about them in like manner, giving themselves over to fornication, and going after strange flesh, are set forth for an example, suffering the vengeance of eternal fire.

God says, *"Having saved the people out of the land of Egypt, afterward destroyed them that believed not."* These angels rebelled against God and are reserved in chains of darkness for the day of judgment. Attention is also called to Sodom and Gomorrah.

We have raised a biblically-illiterate generation with no anchor, no standard, and no moral guide because they have no Bible.

Then He says, *"Likewise."* This means "in the same sense." There are *"filthy dreamers"* alive today in these perilous times. We are living in a filthy age, an age when what was once unmentionable has become common place and is condoned by the masses.

We are called on to be tolerant. We are admonished constantly to accept anything that goes. As a matter of fact, those who cry out for tolerance from those of us who believe the Bible is the Word of God have absolutely no tolerance for us.

God has clearly drawn the lines. It is impossible to have the right standard without the Word of God. A very clever satanic plan has become the order of the day. We have raised a biblically-illiterate generation with no anchor, no standard, and no moral guide because they have no Bible. They are open, accessible, and willing to follow personalities, strange ideas, or almost anything.

We are watching the implosion of the greatest nation on the face of the earth. It is happening before our very eyes. It is the responsibility of the preacher to preach the truth and declare that such things are happening. At the same time, we must remain hopeful in Christ. Can you imagine that when considering all children conceived in our country, one third are born out of wedlock, one third are aborted, and only one third are born into homes with both parents? This is one of the clearest signs of the decay of our nation.

The Bible says in II Timothy 3:13 that *"evil men and seducers shall wax worse and worse."* This means that the world in which we live is going to get worse and worse. As the world gets worse, what we teach and preach from God's Word seems more and more radical–even appearing to be some "off the wall," totally out-of-date set of ideas. In many places, the churches are changing with the world. They may say that they are the same distance from the world that they have always been, but mark how far the world has drifted. *"Evil men and seducers shall wax worse and worse."*

There was a time when every church with the name "Baptist" on the sign would say practically the same thing about the Bible: "We believe the Bible is the Word of God, without error." Something has gone very wrong in this country, but thank God we have the Bible, the Lord Jesus, and the Holy Spirit. We still have the pattern–God's Word!

If there is no truth, if there is no absolute, if people believe there is no God to answer to, it is no wonder they behave the way they do.

I recently read some things in an article from *Newsweek* magazine about a book entitled *The New Voyeurism in America–The Selling of Sex*. Voyeurism has to do with sexual stimulation from viewing things. This is the first generation that has been raised on MTV, music television, and rock video. There is explicit sexual content in these things, not only in pictures but in vocabulary.

One rock performer named Madonna has a book entitled *Sex Celebrating Sadomasochism, Homosexuality, Exhibitionism, and Homoerotica*. She calls herself in the *Newsweek* article a "sexual missionary to change the behavior of our society." She is not the only agent of change. Her behavior is simply a symptom of just how far we have drifted as a nation.

> *We are watching the implosion of the greatest nation on the face of the earth.*

Something must be done! Help is not going to come from Washington, D.C. We have spent too many years believing that we could change the moral standards of our nation by changing the government.

If our nation is going to be helped, she is going to be helped through churches that believe the Bible and speak out the truth. She is going to be helped through homes where people believe the Bible, pray with their children, read the Word of God, and stand for the truth. If she is going to be helped, it will be through Christian institutions that keep the right philosophy before boys and girls and young men and women, a philosophy that grows out of the right theology.

This is the day and hour of greatest responsibility for the church. This is not a time to adjust to the low living around us. We must seize the moment. If you ever intend to be faithful to God, this is the time to do it. If you ever intend to love your church, to be faithful to your church, and to pray for your church and pastor, this is the time to do it. If you ever intend to understand Christian education and promote it, this is the time to do it. The world does not need an imitation of itself. We must hear from God. Pray for revival.

DEFILE THE FLESH

We are living in a world filled with *"filthy dreamers,"* and Jude says they *"defile the flesh."* Speaking of the old world that He destroyed, God says in Genesis 6:5, *"And GOD saw that the wickedness of man was great in the earth, and that every imagination of the thoughts of his heart was only evil continually."*

It was a world that had to be judged. God destroyed the old world with a flood. Only Noah, his wife, his sons, and their wives were spared.

God destroyed the cities of Sodom and Gomorrah by raining fire and brimstone from heaven. The Word of God says in Genesis 19:24-25,

> *Then the LORD rained upon Sodom and upon Gomorrah brimstone and fire from the LORD out of heaven; and he overthrew those cities, and all the plain, and all the inhabitants of the cities, and that which grew upon the ground.*

In human history, the last rung of the ladder is the defiling of the flesh through homosexual behavior and the condoning of it by the general public. Think about this in light of what we have come to in our country. We live in an age of so-called tolerance, which is not tolerance at all. We actually live in an age of indoctrination and anti-God ideas. Truth has been traded for pleasure in the name of tolerance.

The Bible says that these filthy dreamers are characterized by defiling the flesh. The Bible says in Romans 1:21-24,

> *Because that, when they knew God, they glorified him not as God, neither were thankful; but became vain in their imaginations, and their foolish heart was darkened. Professing themselves to be wise, they became fools, and changed the glory of the uncorruptible God into an image made like to corruptible man, and to birds, and fourfooted beasts, and creeping things. Wherefore God also gave them up to uncleanness through the lusts of their own hearts, to dishonour their own bodies between themselves.*

Notice the language, *"God gave them up."* God was not in a situation where He could not control them, judge them, or rain fire from heaven and destroy them. The Bible says that *"God gave them up."*

Imagine a little boy flying a kite. If the kite could speak, it would say, "I wish you would turn me loose. I'd like to be free." We know that if he turns loose of the string, it is not freedom the kite will receive; it is destruction. The string protects the kite. It does not inhibit; it protects. The boundaries protect. The moral guidelines protect and save. When they are gone, it leaves only destruction. God has loosed the string on these people–*"God gave them up."*

The Bible says in verses twenty-five and twenty-six,

> *Who changed the truth of God into a lie, and worshipped and served the creature more than the Creator, who is blessed for ever. Amen. For this cause God gave them up unto vile affections...*

This behavior is not love. God calls it *"vile affections."* An article appeared recently in *USA Today* about two fine-looking young men who are weight lifters. They are handsome fellows who are now married to each other. They go from college campus to college campus lecturing on tolerance in this generation. They say that they are finding the most wonderful reception on college campuses, that people are beginning to understand their rights and their love. As the picture of those handsome young men is fixed in your mind, remember that God calls this *"vile affection."*

> *If our nation is going to be helped, she is going to be helped through churches that believe the Bible and speak out the truth.*

They say, "Oh, you are just an intolerant bigot." If you believe God, stand for truth, and uphold a righteous standard, someone is going to scream at you and call you unloving and unkind. We must lift up our voices and declare the truth in Bible language.

The Bible continues to describe this ungodly behavior in verses twenty-seven and twenty-eight,

> *And likewise also the men, leaving the natural use of the woman, burned in their lust one toward another; men with men working that which is unseemly, and receiving in themselves that recompence of their error which was meet. And even as they did not like to retain God in their knowledge, God gave them over to a reprobate mind.*

They attempted to drive out every thought of God, and God gave them over to a reprobate mind. This is what God is talking about in Jude 8. These *"filthy dreamers"* cannot do right. They look in the face of revealed truth and turn from it, but their minds are filled with everything but pleasant, pure thoughts.

I have thought about this many times as I have counseled with people who have harmed their bodies through sinful, sexual behavior. There is a sexual bonding, but it is not a bonding of love. Most people today do not understand love. Love is a decision, not an emotion. Love is a commitment, not an emotion. People do not understand that there are different kinds of bonding that bring people together.

Notice carefully what God says about immorality in Proverbs 5:1-13,

> *My son, attend unto my wisdom, and bow thine ear to my understanding: that thou mayest regard discretion, and that thy lips may keep knowledge. For the lips of a strange woman drop as an honeycomb, and her mouth is smoother than oil.*

The word *"strange"* means "that which does not belong to you."

> *But her end is bitter as wormwood, sharp as a twoedged sword. Her feet go down to death; her steps take hold on hell. Lest thou shouldest ponder the path of life, her ways are moveable, that thou canst not know them. Hear me now therefore, O ye children, and depart not from the words of my mouth. Remove thy way far from her, and come not nigh the door of her house: Lest thou give thine honour unto others, and thy years unto the cruel: lest strangers be filled with thy wealth; and thy labours be in the house of a stranger; and thou mourn at the last, when thy flesh and thy body are consumed. And say, How have I hated instruction, and my heart despised reproof; and have not obeyed the voice of my teachers, nor inclined mine ear to them that instructed me!*

In our Bible-believing churches, we must be willing to do whatever is necessary to uphold the standard of the Word of God and get God's message out.

A dear mother who came to Christ recently said to me, "Pastor, I don't know the Bible. I don't know the teachings of the Bible. I don't know how to raise my children. I don't know how to discipline my children. Show me these things from the Bible, and I will do them."

People do not know the Word of God. By the thousands and thousands, people are destroying themselves by defiling their flesh. We must work to win the lost and teach them God's Word.

DESPISE DOMINION

These *"filthy dreamers"* want no one telling them what to do.

Without Christ, men attempt to decide who they will master. As Christians, we must yield our lives to Christ and allow Him to be our Master.

The Bible says in Psalm 2:1-3,

> *Why do the heathen rage, and the people imagine a vain thing? The kings of the earth set themselves, and the rulers take counsel together, against the LORD, and against his anointed, saying, Let us break their bands asunder, and cast away their cords from us.*

The unsaved world says in the face of God, "No one is going to tell us what to do. No one is going to rule over us. No one is going to be our boss." Christian people who are discouraged need to realize that this has not shaken God.

The Bible says in verses four through six,

> *He that sitteth in the heavens shall laugh: the Lord shall have them in derision. Then shall he speak unto them in his wrath, and vex them in his sore displeasure. Yet have I set my king upon my holy hill of Zion.*

We are living in an age of anarchy. An anarchist does what is right in his own eyes. All of these things simply bring us a step closer to the coming of Jesus Christ.

Some day, stepping on the stage of human history will be someone who appears to be a benevolent dictator who will promise to solve all the world's problems. That person will be the Antichrist. Our world is getting ready for him.

Where does this leave us? We still have God's Word and God's promises. Heaven is our home. The community of the saved is still intact. We are still to be a holy minority in the midst of an unholy majority. We are declaring the truth and standing for righteousness.

We must understand what we are dealing with today. We have gone through a mental revolution in our world. Millions of people do not think the way they once thought. Do we throw in the towel and give up? No! We are needed now more than ever.

> *We do not live in a day of opportunity. We live in a day of responsibility, and everyone of God's children must seek the Lord for the strength needed for the task at hand.*

The Bible standard must be the standard taken by God's people in every generation. If you remember in Genesis chapter three, the Devil said certain things to Adam and Eve. One thing he said was: "You are going to know good and evil. You won't need anyone telling you what is right and what is wrong. You are going to know what is right and wrong." The Bible says that this crowd in Jude 8 despises dominion. No one tells them what to do. This is certainly the spirit of our age.

SPEAK EVIL OF DIGNITIES

The word *"dignities"* means "those to whom honor is due." In this age, people speak evil of those who are to be honored. Who are these people?

God's Word says in Ephesians 6:2, *"Honour thy father and mother."* We are living in a day when children can divorce their parents. Did you ever think we would have such a thing in our country? Now we have lawsuits in which children successfully divorce their parents.

I understand that child abuse is a very grave problem. My heart is stirred as I think about children being abused—verbally, physically, and sexually. May God help us because honor for parents in the home is a disappearing thing. Children are being taught that they may have to listen to their parents for a little while, but they do not have to agree with them.

One of the great things about Christian education is the work done with the family. For no reason would a true Christian educator take a position against the home. Everything is done to strengthen the home.

These *"filthy dreamers"* speak evil of those in churches. The brunt of many jokes today is the leader in the church. I have seen in my lifetime how people have made preachers appear a dime a dozen. Many ministers have done things that have cheapened the office of the ministry and destroyed the respect that people had, but there are still thousands of good men in the ministry who believe God's Word and are trying to live right.

Uphold your pastor, pray for him, and strengthen him in the Lord. It is your responsibility. It is wrong to criticize the preacher or anyone else who is trying to help your family with things that are righteous.

My heart has been broken by people who have dishonored the ministry and have done immoral things. People seldom get over that kind of sin. Churches may never fully recover from it. There should be respect, love, and honor for people who are trying to serve God.

This matter of speaking evil of dignities goes all the way to God. People have no fear of God before their eyes. Many comedians would just as soon crack a joke about God as anything else. To them, God is some weak, feeble old man unable to cope with the increasingly difficult problems of our land.

"These filthy dreamers defile the flesh, despise dominion, and speak evil of dignities." We live in this kind of world. Someone may say, "I would like to go to some other country in the world where it is not this way." There is no such place. Instead, let us make a difference in the world in which we live. May God help us to take the right stand with the right spirit. It is not what I can do, but rather what God can do through me. We do not live in a day of opportunity. We live in a day of responsibility, and everyone of God's children must seek the Lord for the strength needed for the task at hand.

"Yet Michael the archangel, when contending with the devil he disputed about the body of Moses, durst not bring against him a railing accusation, but said, The Lord rebuke thee."

Jude 9

CHAPTER SIX

THE LORD REBUKE THEE

 e have learned that our Lord desires for us to earnestly contend for the faith which was once delivered unto the saints. These are difficult days. We forget that we are dealing with the Devil. The Devil comes disguised. Satan comes through deceptive means, but we need to be aware that there is supernatural power involved in the opposition that we face. There is a battle raging around us and inside us. We can have the victory only through our Lord.

In the eighth verse, God characterized these filthy dreamers by saying that they defile the flesh, they despise dominion, and they speak evil of dignities. Just ahead, the Bible says in verse nine, *"Yet Michael the archangel, when contending with the devil he disputed about the body of Moses, durst not bring against him a railing accusation, but said, The Lord rebuke thee."*

Many read this verse and think, "This is a proof text for not dealing with the Devil." In reality, it is more than this. In this verse, God is dealing with apostates who speak evil of dignities, who speak against those in authority. The Lord takes for example that even the archangel Michael did not bring a railing accusation against the Devil but committed him to the Lord.

From this passage, we know clearly that we need strength and power from the Lord to deal with the Devil; there is also a solemn warning in this verse that we should not bring accusations against those in authority. Notice again the eighth and ninth verses,

> *Likewise also these filthy dreamers defile the flesh, despise dominion, and speak evil of dignities. Yet Michael the archangel, when contending with the devil he disputed about the body of Moses, durst not bring against him a railing accusation, but said, The Lord rebuke thee.*

Some people believe that having a tongue and the ability to use it is a license to destroy people.

Notice that God uses the definite article here. He says, *"Michael the archangel."* There is only one archangel.

In the twelfth chapter of the Revelation of Jesus Christ, we find that Michael had the power to deal with the Devil. The Bible says in Revelation 12:7, *"And there was war in heaven: Michael and his angels fought against the dragon; and the dragon fought and his angels."* There was a battle between Michael the archangel and Lucifer, and between the angels of Michael and the angels of Lucifer. The Bible says in Revelation 12:8, *"And prevailed not; neither was their place found any more in heaven."* Lucifer and his angels did not prevail against Michael.

You might say it was the archangel's privilege and responsibility to rebuke the Devil, but God says that Michael the archangel did not do this, but committed it to the Lord. This does not mean that we are not to tell people where they have erred, but it does mean that we should show them what God's Word says.

The point is, there is a proper way to deal with those in authority. The warning is against tearing down those in authority. From this, the Lord leads us right into the sin of Core and the criticism of Moses' authority.

Some people believe that having a tongue and the ability to use it is a license to destroy people. None of us are careful enough concerning those we talk about and what we say. May God convict us to commit these things to Him. We should turn people over to the Lord and stop trying to be God and attempting to execute judgment on people, when even the archangel would not do such a thing to the Devil.

THE EVIL THAT SURROUNDS US

Looking back at Jude 9, make note that the Bible says, *"Yet Michael the archangel, when contending with the devil he disputed about the body of Moses, durst not bring against him a railing accusation, but said, The Lord rebuke thee."*

We are surrounded by evil. This should prepare us for a life of prayer and faith in God.

The Bible teaches that we are contending with the Devil. There is a battle going on. This particular contention in the book of Jude had to do with Moses' body. The Devil must have had some sort of plan. It is purely speculative to think of what he was going to do with the body of Moses.

This passage from Jude is the only time in the Bible that the contention over the body of Moses is mentioned. It is not mentioned at the time of Moses' death but evidently has reference to some period of time immediately following Moses' death.

There are other things like this in the Word of God. For example, there are things that the Lord Jesus said which are quoted in the New Testament record but are not given in the Gospel records. In II Timothy chapter three the names of those who withstood Moses, Jannes and Jambres, are given to us, but they are not given in the Old Testament account.

Here, by divine revelation, God tells us that an incident took place in which there was contention regarding the body of Moses between Michael the archangel and the Devil. The Bible says in Deuteronomy 34:5-8,

> *So Moses the servant of the LORD died there in the land of Moab, according to the word of the LORD. And he buried him in a valley in the land of Moab, over against Beth-peor: but no man knoweth of his sepulchre unto this day. And Moses was an hundred and twenty years old when he died: his eye was not dim, nor his natural force abated. And the children of Israel wept for Moses in the plains of Moab thirty days: so the days of weeping and mourning for Moses were ended.*

When Moses died, God buried him. The children of Israel did not see his body, and they were not involved in the burial of his body. God buried him, and no man knows where he is buried.

The Bible says that there was spiritual contention over the death, the burial, and the body of Moses. The point I would like to make to you is that there is always evil surrounding us and evil contention going on round about. Most of the time, we are unaware of it.

Many believe that the Devil wanted the body of Moses in order to make an idol of it and deceive the children of Israel into worshiping the image of Moses and turning from the Lord. This type of thing is found in other places.

Speaking of the Antichrist, the thirteenth chapter of the Revelation of Jesus Christ says in verses three and four,

> *And I saw one of his heads as it were wounded to death; and his deadly wound was healed: and all the world wondered after the beast. And they worshipped the dragon which gave power unto the beast: and they worshipped the beast, saying, Who is like unto the beast? who is able to make war with him?*

The Devil had some plan concerning the body of Moses. We know that during the Tribulation period some deadly wound will be inflicted upon the Beast, yet he will be revived in some way and worshiped. The Devil will also be worshiped. Let us not be ignorant of his devices.

May God help us to be aware that there is evil all around us. Spiritual warfare is raging.

THE ENEMY WHO SEEKS TO HARM US

The second thing we see in this Bible text is that the enemy seeks to harm us. The Bible clearly identifies the Devil in verse nine, *"Yet Michael the archangel, when contending with the devil."* This is the enemy that seeks to harm us. It is entirely possible to talk about the awful condition of our world and give statistical information that references many of the evils of our society and still miss the point.

> *The Devil does not do his dirtiest, most destructive work with shameful acts that the world thinks of as awful. He does his most destructive work in deceiving people through some religious means.*

For example, more than four hundred different pornographic magazines are published every month in America. One million, five hundred thousand babies are murdered in America on a yearly basis. As many as 30,000 children a month are filmed in pornographic movies. Morality and decency are being destroyed. The Devil is behind it, but I do not believe the Devil is most proud of that. There are five thousand new people who start using cocaine every day in America, but I do not believe the Devil is most proud of that.

Satan is most proud of his work done in religious deception. People are damned because they believe something other than the plain truth that Jesus Christ is the only way to heaven. Every day I live I am more and more grateful that God has led me to be a Bible-believing Christian. We declare boldly and happily that Jesus Christ is the only way to heaven. We work to take the message of the gospel to everyone, and Satan tries to hinder us in this effort.

The first time the archangel Michael was mentioned in the Bible, he was dealing with the Devil. In the Old Testament, as Daniel prayed, God spoke to him. This passage of Scripture should wake us up as we think of the enemy who seeks to harm us. The Bible says in Daniel 10:12-13,

> *Then said he unto me, Fear not, Daniel: for from the first day that thou didst set thine heart to understand, and to chasten thyself before thy God, thy words were heard, and I am come for thy words. But the prince of the kingdom of Persia withstood me one and twenty days: but, lo, Michael, one of the chief princes, came to help me; and I remained there with the kings of Persia.*

Daniel's prayer was hindered for twenty-one days by this prince of Persia until Michael intervened. What we cannot see is as real as what we see. If the curtain could be pulled back and we could see the spirit world, we would witness a real warfare of spirit beings.

Our world has become a garden of strange gods.

So many scoff at the idea of a real Devil and a real God. Can you imagine a man praying for twenty-one days and his answer being withstood by some general in the Devil's army? The Bible says in Ephesians 6:10-12,

> *Finally, my brethren, be strong in the Lord, and in the power of his might. Put on the whole armour of God, that ye may be able to stand against the wiles of the devil. For we wrestle not against flesh and blood, but against principalities, against powers, against the rulers*

of the darkness of this world, against spiritual wickedness in high places.

We are told in Revelation 12:4 that as many as one-third of the angels rebelled against God with Satan. Some of those fallen angels are reserved in chains until the day of judgment. Others of those fallen angels are loose with the Devil, the god of this world, the prince and power of the air, to wage war against God and God's children. We refer to these fallen angels as demons.

> *When dealing with authority, this verse teaches that we need to commit it to the Lord, and not take it into our hands. It is a shame that many of us try to play God with other people's lives.*

The Bible teaches that they operate a well-organized force of evil. There are certain evil commanders and evil leaders, spirit beings, who have assignments to disrupt the work of God.

Oh, how we need the Lord Jesus Christ! The Devil does not do his dirtiest, most destructive work with shameful acts that the world thinks of as awful. He does his most destructive work in deceiving people through some religious means.

God gives us a warning in I John 4:1. The Bible says, *"Beloved, believe not every spirit, but try the spirits whether they are of God: because many false prophets are gone out into the world."* We need discernment from the Holy Spirit to discern the spirits.

Our world has become a garden of strange gods. We meet all kinds of folks who talk about gods, spirits, spirit beings, channels, spirit guides, masters, and use many types of religious expressions. The Bible says that we need the Holy Spirit to discern the truth. Behind all these evil spirits is the Devil. As our enemy, he seeks to harm us.

THE EVERLASTING REFUGE WE HAVE IN OUR LORD

The third thing we find in Jude 9 is the everlasting refuge we have in our Lord. The Bible says, *"Yet Michael the archangel, when contending with the devil he disputed about the body of Moses, durst not bring against him a railing accusation, but said, The Lord rebuke thee."*

In this passage, Michael commits Satan to the Lord. Our refuge is the Lord God Almighty. The hardest thing to do in life is to determine the human from the divine. We have brains, bodies, muscles, and other abilities. We can see, hear, smell, feel, and taste. What are we to do, and what is God to do? We must distinguish our ideas from God's ideas.

When dealing with authority, this verse teaches that we need to commit it to the Lord, and not take it into our hands. It is a shame that many of us try to play God with other people's lives. If there is a clear, definite guideline in the Word of God, give people the verse and commit it to the Lord.

Every human being is a soul for whom Christ died, a person God created. God wants to do a spiritual work in each life. Christian people should walk with the Lord and leave things in God's hands.

The Bible records that Michael said to Lucifer, *"The Lord rebuke thee."* Our refuge is the Lord, not just from evil and harm, but from attempting to do more than God wants us to do. The most taxing thing on human life is assuming God's responsibility. We often admit that things are out of our hands and that we are not going to be able to change people's hearts, but we continue wrestling with it.

I have had to learn as a father and a pastor that God by His Holy Spirit can convict, lead, work, and do things that I am not capable of doing. I can be used of God by committing these things to the Lord. If I do not commit them to God, I will not be used of God.

We all agree that we are surrounded by an evil conspiracy, a spirit world, and a raging battle. There is an evil one behind it all. We cannot stand in our own strength. God is our refuge and our strength.

Holy angels and unholy angels are not out somewhere having sword fights to see who is the best. The battle rages over the souls of men.

None of us are as aware as we should be that God wants to use us as vehicles to point people to Jesus Christ. Either we are going to be used of God or used of the Devil.

Our only everlasting refuge is to cast ourselves at the mercy of Jesus Christ and ask God to use us and direct us. Someone is battling for your home. Someone is battling for your spouse. Someone is battling for your mind. Someone is battling for your children. Someone is battling for your school. Someone is battling for your church. Someone is battling for your Sunday School class. Someone is battling for your baby. Someone is battling for everything you love dearly. We need to make sure that we are being used of God in this battle by casting ourselves on the mercy of God, trusting in the Lord, and being filled with the Word of God.

Michael the archangel said, *"The Lord rebuke thee."* I can tell if I am walking in the Spirit of the Lord by the way I react to things. If I react properly by looking for God's hand in my circumstances, trusting God to use me, asking the Holy Spirit to guide me, and finding God's Word to help and strengthen me, then the Lord can get glory in every situation. If I do not depend on the Lord and look to His Word, then He cannot get the glory.

Our churches must awaken to the spiritual conflict. As God's people, we must say, "Lord, be our everlasting Refuge."

We once lived in a house with a big field in our backyard. We had a little dog named Shamus. Just down from us was a ferocious, monstrous German shepherd. I was scared of the dog, but if I happened to be near my house, I could scare that big dog away.

On one particular occasion, my little dog was in the field behind our house, and that big German shepherd came through. My little dog was scared to death. I started yelling at that German shepherd. When the big dog saw me, he started running as fast as he could run. My little

> *The most taxing thing on human life is assuming God's responsibility.*

dog started chasing him. After a while, my dog turned around and pranced back, as if to say, "Look what I did."

I thought to myself, "I would like to communicate with you if I could. I would like for you to know, that dog could devour you with one bite. You could not stay alive around him for thirty seconds. You think you scared off that big dog. The truth is that you did not scare him off at all. I ran him off."

Think of the times we have been lifted up in pride–thinking we had accomplished such great things. The Lord wants to say, "I would like to explain something to you if you would listen. That victory was not won by your effort. I gave you that victory. I took care of that for you because I love you."

Even the archangel said, *"The Lord rebuke thee."* Many of us need to come again to the feet of the Lord Jesus and say, "Lord, I need Thee. I know that I am not going to have the spiritual victory apart from Thee."

"But these speak evil of those things which they know not: but what they know naturally, as brute beasts, in those things they corrupt themselves. Woe unto them! for they have gone in the way of Cain, and ran greedily after the error of Balaam for reward, and perished in the gainsaying of Core."

Jude 10-11

CHAPTER SEVEN

BRUTE BEASTS

There are times when we discover things in the Word of God that seem shocking. This is an instance when God uses a rather shocking term for these people. The Bible says in Jude 10-11,

> *But these speak evil of those things which they know not: but what they know naturally, as brute beasts, in those things they corrupt themselves. Woe unto them! for they have gone in the way of Cain, and ran greedily after the error of Balaam for reward, and perished in the gainsaying of Core.*

God calls these people *"brute beasts."* They are religious animals.

When reading this particular passage, keep in mind that we are dealing with apostates. We are not dealing with people who are normally thought of by others as evil. We are not dealing with people who would be categorized as the lower types in the world, the criminal element and the low life, but God says these people are *"brute beasts."*

There is the natural man, and there is the spiritual man. There are saved people, and there are unsaved people. A man who does not know the Lord Jesus Christ as his Savior works entirely with the natural. He understands nothing about the spiritual. God says these people who talk about religious things and declare that they know almost everything about every subject are really operating entirely on the natural and know nothing of the spiritual. They are *"brute beasts."*

You may realize that you are acquainted with some of these *"brute beasts,"* and I hope you understand more fully why they behave the way they do.

The Bible says in I Corinthians 2:14, *"But the natural man receiveth not the things of the Spirit of God: for they are foolishness unto him: neither can he know them, because they are spiritually discerned."* The Bible says that the natural man cannot know the things of God. It is impossible for a man who has never been born of the Spirit of God, no matter how religious he may appear to be or how much he may talk about God, to understand anything about the work of the Spirit of God. These are *"brute beasts."*

We live in a very religious world. It is popular to be religious.

I read an article recently about a well-known personality from our state who plants trees in his yard, and he believes he gains spiritual insight from walking among these trees. For this man, who happens to be the former Vice President of the United States, it is a religious endeavor to be near those trees. Can you imagine such a thing? This man would not deny the existence of God, but he would declare God to be something that He is not. If he has never been born of the Spirit of God, no matter how intelligent he may appear, the Lord says he is a *"brute beast."*

While recently flying to speak at a Christian college, I started a conversation with a man seated next to me who listened for a moment until I confronted him about whether or not he knew Jesus Christ as his personal Savior. Rather boisterously he said to me, "I'm not for any of that. I don't believe in God. I don't believe in the things you are talking about concerning God." He went on to tell me what degrees he had earned, and he started to explain some things he thought I needed to know.

He had the idea that I would accept everything he said as fact because of his education. He talked to me as if I were listening to someone I was greatly interested in hearing and believed everything he was saying. Finally, I was able to declare to him that the Bible says in Psalm 14:1, *"The fool hath said in his heart, There is no God."* I want to be kind, but it makes no difference how much you know. If you do not know the Lord, the Bible says you are a fool.

It is impossible for a man who has never been born of the Spirit of God, no matter how religious he may appear to be or how much he may talk about God, to understand anything about the work of the Spirit of God.

What we preach and teach from the Word of God is divisive. Truth reveals. If the world really is divided between the lost and the saved, and we speak the message of God by the Spirit of God, do we realize that only those who have spiritual understanding are going to understand our message?

God declares in verse ten of Jude that these brute beasts not only speak what is natural, they also speak about *"those things which they know not."* Here the self-declared intelligent are told that they do not know anything about which they speak. People enjoy talking about God, but the Bible says in verse four, *"For there are certain men crept in unawares, who were before of old ordained to this condemnation, ungodly men."*

BRUTE BEASTS DO NOT KNOW GOD

To be *"ungodly"* means to refuse to submit to God's authority. The Bible says in verse ten that they speak about *"those things which they know not."* They talk about God and about religion, but they do not even know God.

BRUTE BEASTS DO NOT HAVE SALVATION

Another thing they like to talk about but do not know is salvation. The Bible says in verse four, speaking of this same crowd, that they have turned *"the grace of our God into lasciviousness."* They have turned *"the grace of our God"* into a license to sin. This is unleashed sexual desire; it is doing anything they feel like doing. This means that they do not understand anything about salvation. The Bible says in Ephesians 2:8-9, *"For by grace are ye saved through faith; and that not of yourselves: it is the gift of God: Not of works, lest any man should boast."*

There is only one way to be saved. That one way is by the grace of God through faith. These people speak about God, but they do not know God because they will not submit to God. They speak about salvation and the things of God, but they are not saved. They have turned the grace of God into lasciviousness.

BRUTE BEASTS DO NOT KNOW THE LORD JESUS CHRIST

The Bible says in the closing part of verse four that they are *"denying the only Lord God, and our Lord Jesus Christ."* They do not know the Lord Jesus Christ, but they talk about Him. They know the historical figure, Jesus Christ, but they do not know the biblical Christ. Christ became man without ceasing to be God, yet without sin.

The longer we live, the more we are going to hear from this religious crowd who talks about God but does not know Him. They talk about salvation but know nothing about it. They discuss Jesus Christ, but they do not know Him because they are depending entirely upon the natural.

The point of the passage is very simple. God has a way, and man has a way. God's way is the right way, the best way, and the only way. Remember that Proverbs 14:12 says that *"there is a way which seemeth right unto a man."* He is willing to argue that his way is the right way.

> *A bloodless, Christless religion still leaves man a lost sinner.*

If we are born again people, if we have spiritual life from God, if we live by faith, then we must admit that the unsaved know nothing of the new birth. The unsaved do not understand the spiritual life or the Spirit of God. The unsaved do not understand the faith life. So often, even as

Christians, we condescend to the world's ways and do not live like citizens of heaven should live in this world.

God warns us. Remember that God has a way, and man has a way. We need to be absolutely sure that we are going God's way. Notice verses ten and eleven,

> *But these speak evil of those things which they know not: but what they know naturally, as brute beasts, in those things they corrupt themselves. Woe unto them! for they have gone in the way of Cain, and ran greedily after the error of Balaam for reward, and perished in the gainsaying of Core.*

For us to understand this, we need to look at the way of Cain, the error of Balaam, and the gainsaying of Core. May the Spirit of God turn His light on our lives as we look at these Bible stories.

THE WAY OF CAIN

Let us look at the way of Cain in Genesis chapter four. We know the story of creation. We know that God created man and woman and placed them in the Garden of Eden. From the dust of the earth, God made Adam. God then caused a deep sleep to come upon Adam, took out a rib, and made woman.

It appears that they were not in the garden long before they sinned. After they sinned against God, they hid themselves. They were clothed in the glory of God before their sin. There was a garment of glory about them.

When they sinned, the innocence was gone, and sin entered into the bloodstream of all humanity through our first parents.

The Bible says in Romans 5:12, *"Wherefore, as by one man sin entered into the world, and death by sin; and so death passed upon all men, for that all have sinned."* They looked at themselves and saw that they were naked. They hid themselves and made garments of fig leaves to hide their nakedness. God came to them in the cool of the day, walking in the garden, crying out, *"Adam, where art thou?"*

God made for them coats of skin. The Bible says in Genesis 3:21, *"Unto Adam also and to his wife did the LORD God make coats of skins, and clothed them."* An innocent animal was slain for the guilty Adam and Eve. The blood was shed, making the way to God the blood way. The natural brute beast does not understand this. To him, it is a "butcher religion." It is offensive to the natural mind. In many places today, preachers are no longer preaching the blood way. But the only way to God is through the Lord Jesus Christ and His shed blood on the cross.

God blessed Adam and Eve with sons. The Bible says in Genesis 4:1-5,

> *And Adam knew Eve his wife; and she conceived, and bare Cain, and said, I have gotten a man from the LORD. And she again bare his brother Abel. And Abel was a keeper of sheep, but Cain was a tiller of the ground. And in process of time it came to pass, that Cain brought of the fruit of the ground an offering unto the LORD. And Abel, he also brought of the firstlings of his flock and of the fat thereof. And the LORD had respect unto Abel and to his offering: But unto Cain and to his offering he had not respect. And Cain was very wroth, and his countenance fell.*

When these men came before the Lord, God had already revealed that the way to God was the blood way. Abel was willing to acknowledge that there was sin and that there needed to be a sacrifice for atonement. Abel was willing to submit himself to God and confess the need he had in his life. What God had revealed was that man was a sinner. He needed a Savior, a substitute, the innocent for the guilty.

Cain gathered the best of his crop, and it seemed to him like a good thing. The Bible says in Genesis 4:3, *"And in process of time it came to pass, that Cain brought of the fruit of the ground an offering unto the LORD."* To the natural man, it seemed like a very good thing. This is religion without Christ. A bloodless, Christless religion still leaves man a lost sinner.

> *No one on the face of the earth has a greater accountability and responsibility to God than the God-called preacher.*

The way of Cain is a refusal to submit to the way of God. The way of Cain is a proud way that says, "It is my way, not God's way." It is heartbreaking that so many people in churches are not hearing the simple truth of salvation. We would be shocked to know the number of preachers who cannot explain to people how to be saved. If they do not teach that the only way to God is through what Jesus Christ accomplished on the cross of Calvary with His death, burial, and resurrection from the dead, no wonder they are pointing people religiously to hell.

I was visiting in a hospital recently, witnessing to a dear little lady. Her priest had been by to see her. She was seriously ill. She and her priest had been discussing the giving of absolution for her sins, something a man, her priest, claimed to be able to do. My heart was hurting because I realized that what she needed is what all people need. Only God can forgive our sin debt.

The Bible says that these religious brute beasts have gone the way of Cain. May God help us to get the gospel to people. We are such hypocrites when we sit in a church, saying "amen" to the preaching of the truth, yet we do not tell people how to be saved. We should preach it in the church, but people also need to hear it where they are. May God help us to go to the ends of the earth with the gospel. The Lord Jesus Christ is the only way to heaven.

THE ERROR OF BALAAM

The Bible says in the book of Jude that not only have they gone the way of Cain, but they have run *"greedily after the error of Balaam."* Balaam is mentioned many times in the Word of God. We find the doctrine of Balaam, the way of Balaam, and the error of Balaam. The Bible says they *"ran greedily after the error of Balaam."*

In Bible times, on the east side of Jordan, there were certain areas of land divided by rivers. These rivers ran east and west and provided northern and southern borders for certain people.

One such portion of ground belonged to the Moabites. As the children of Israel traveled in that land, they came near these Moabite people. The Bible says in Numbers 22:1-7,

> *And the children of Israel set forward, and pitched in the plains of Moab on this side Jordan by Jericho. And Balak the son of Zippor saw all that Israel had done to the Amorites. And Moab was sore afraid of the people, because they were*

many: and Moab was distressed because of the children of Israel. And Moab said unto the elders of Midian, Now shall this company lick up all that are round about us, as the ox licketh up the grass of the field. And Balak the son of Zippor was king of the Moabites at that time. He sent messengers therefore unto Balaam the son of Beor to Pethor, which is by the river of the land of the children of his people, to call him, saying, Behold, there is a people come out from Egypt: behold, they cover the face of the earth, and they abide over against me: come now therefore, I pray thee, curse me this people; for they are too mighty for me: peradventure I shall prevail, that we may smite them, and that I may drive them out of the land: for I wot that he whom thou blessest is blessed, and he whom thou cursest is cursed. And the elders of Moab and the elders of Midian departed with the rewards of divination in their hand; and they came unto Balaam, and spake unto him the words of Balak.

The Jewish people are a blessed people, a people with a special purpose on the earth. To them and through them the Lord chose to make Himself known to the rest of the world.

As the Jews traveled near the Moabites, King Balak said, "Find Balaam." The King was evidently an unbelieving person who knew very little about the Jews. "Find him, and we will reward him. We will give him things if he will curse the Jews."

Balaam heard this request from Balak, and he went to God. The Bible says in Numbers 22:12-13,

And God said unto Balaam, Thou shalt not go with them; thou shalt not curse the people: for they are blessed. And Balaam rose up in the morning, and said unto the princes of Balak, Get you into your land: for the LORD refuseth to give me leave to go with you.

It was a settled matter. God said no, but they came again to Balaam. The Bible says in verse seventeen, *"For I will promote thee unto very great honour, and I will do whatsoever thou sayest unto me: come therefore, I pray thee, curse me this people."*

After God said no, they approached Balaam again. Balaam wanted the reward. He wanted that promotion. The greed inside him would not let him stop. This was the error of Balaam. As a hireling, he went on. He was willing to be hired in his service, failing to realize that God had a special covenant purpose for Israel.

According to Dr. A. T. Pierson, a famous Bible teacher of a century ago,

> The...real character and vile conspiracy are only hinted in the narrative in Numbers (22:31). But the comments of Peter, Jude and John lend new meaning to the whole story (2 Pet. 2:15; Jude 1:11; Rev. 2:14). Thus not until we turn to the last of the sixty-six books, the very close of the whole volume of Scripture, do we know how much this soothsayer of Mesopotamia had to do with that awful plunge of Jehovah's people into the abyss of sensuality. In Numbers, the facts are registered of their sin and crime, followed by an obscure hint of Balaam's complicity with it; but the Apocalypse finally withdraws the veil and discloses his full agency as the chief conspirator.

The word *"stumblingblock"* in Revelation 2:14 means, literally, that part of a trap wherein bait is laid, and which, when touched by the animal as it seizes the bait, caused the trap to spring and shut so as to catch the prey. What a darkly suggestive word to describe that human bait of female charms that made this trip so seductively effectual! Here also for the first time, we learn that Balaam set a double snare, entangling Israel in idolatry as well as immorality.

And so, after many centuries, evil reappears in its older forms and complications. As Balak and the Moabites had literally been Balaam's followers and accomplices in encouraging idol sacrifices and sensual sins, so the Pergamites had in both forms followed Balaam's doctrine and accompanied these literal sins of the flesh by spiritual idolatry and adultery, corrupting the worship of God, and encouraging infidelity to the sacred bridal vows of the church to the heavenly Bridegroom!

The Lord Jesus Christ said in John chapter ten that there is a difference between the hireling and the shepherd. God warns us in the book of Jude that these apostates are people who are for hire. The hireling flees because he does not care for the sheep.

THE GAINSAYING OF CORE

The third warning concerns the gainsaying of Core. The Bible says that they *"perished in the gainsaying of Core."* We find the rebellion of Core or *"Korah"* in the book of Numbers. It was a rebellion against Aaron the high priest and Moses. Korah, Moses, and Aaron were from the same tribe, the tribe of Levi. The Bible says in Numbers 16:1-3,

Now Korah, the son of Izhar, the son of Kohath, the son of Levi, and Dathan and Abiram, the sons of Eliab, and On, the son of Peleth, sons of Reuben, took men: and they rose up before Moses, with certain of the children of Israel, two hundred and fifty princes of the assembly, famous in the congregation, men of renown: and they gathered themselves together against Moses and against Aaron, and said unto them, Ye take too much upon you, seeing all the congregation are holy, every one of them, and the LORD is among them: wherefore then lift ye up yourselves above the congregation of the LORD?

They gathered themselves together against Moses and Aaron. Notice the action of Moses. The Bible says in verse four, *"And when Moses heard it, he fell upon his face."* He did not say, "Come outside and let's fight it out." He did not get into a screaming match with him. He did not try to fight back. He did not run and tell someone how evil Korah happened to be. He fell on his face, acknowledging that he was turning to the Lord with this difficulty. The Bible continues in verses five through nine,

And he spake unto Korah and unto all his company, saying, Even to morrow the LORD will shew who are his, and who is holy; and will cause him to come near unto him: even him whom he hath chosen will he cause to come near unto him. This do; take you censers, Korah, and all his company; and put fire therein, and put incense in them before the LORD to morrow: and it shall be that the man whom the LORD doth choose, he shall be holy: ye take too much upon you, ye sons of Levi. And Moses said unto Korah, Hear, I pray you, ye sons of Levi: seemeth it but a small thing

unto you, that the God of Israel hath separated you from the congregation of Israel, to bring you near to himself to do the service of the tabernacle of the LORD, and to stand before the congregation to minister unto them?

They were of the tribe of Levi. Moses said, "Does it mean nothing to you that you have the privilege to serve God? Does it mean nothing to you that God has chosen you to carry the instruments of the tabernacle of God?" The Bible says in verse ten, *"And he hath brought thee near to him, and all thy brethren the sons of Levi with thee: and seek ye the priesthood also?"*

Moses said, "It is not enough. You want the office of the priesthood that Aaron holds also, don't you?" He continues in verse eleven, *"For which cause both thou and all thy company are gathered together against the LORD."* He does not say, "against Moses." He does not say, "against Aaron." He says, *"against the LORD."*

God calls men into the ministry. No one on the face of the earth has a greater accountability and responsibility to God than the God-called preacher. No one walks in such severe judgment before God as does the God-called preacher. The God-called preacher is God's man. He is the Lord's anointed.

When a church extends an invitation to a pastor, that church acknowledges that they believe God wants that man to be the pastor of their church. When anyone rebels against this, he is really rebelling against God.

In many places people have entered into the gainsaying of Core. There is a severe word from God for this crowd.

The Bible says in verse eleven, *"And what is Aaron, that ye murmur against him?"* What they really wanted was Aaron's job. The Bible continues in verses twelve and thirteen,

> *And Moses sent to call Dathan and Abiram, the sons of Eliab: which said, We will not come up: Is it a small thing that thou hast brought us into a land that floweth with milk and honey, to kill us in the wilderness, except thou make thyself altogether a prince over us?*

Moses did not appoint himself as a prince over the people. Did he walk all the way from the wilderness in the backside of the desert to Pharaoh's court and ask God for this responsibility? No. God spoke to Moses through the burning bush and said, "I want you to do it." Moses said, "I can't." Every God-called preacher has said to the Lord, "God, I am not able." God said, "Go, and I will make you able." That is what Moses did. He went in the strength of the Lord, and God enabled him.

The people began to accuse Moses in verses fourteen through seventeen,

> *Moreover thou hast not brought us into a land that floweth with milk and honey, or given us inheritance of fields and vineyards: wilt thou put out the eyes of these men? we will not come up. And Moses was very wroth, and said unto the LORD, Respect not thou their offering: I have not taken one ass from them, neither have I hurt one of them. And Moses said unto Korah, Be thou and all thy company before the LORD, thou, and they, and Aaron, to morrow: and take every man his censer, and put incense in them, and bring ye before the LORD every man his censer,*

two hundred and fifty censers; thou also, and Aaron, each of you his censer.

Core had gathered 250 princes of the assembly who were famous in the congregation, men of renown. It is a wonderful thing when God touches a man, touches his home, touches his family, and gives him responsibility in the work of the Lord. It is an awesome responsibility to be one of the renowned–to be a person with influence in the work of the Lord. But oh, what a responsibility to use that influence wisely!

May the Lord help us to identify *"the way of Cain, the error of Balaam, and the gainsaying of Core"* and to determine to follow the Lord Jesus Christ with all our hearts. Cain refused to come to God the blood way. We need to continue to preach that salvation is only through the blood of Jesus Christ. Balaam was for hire. He lived to please men and to promote himself. We should serve the Lord out of a desire to please Him and Him alone. Core rebelled against authority that was appointed by God. Let us follow those the Lord has given to us who provide leadership in the work of God.

"These are spots in your feasts of charity, when they feast with you, feeding themselves without fear: clouds they are without water, carried about of winds; trees whose fruit withereth, without fruit, twice dead, plucked up by the roots; Raging waves of the sea, foaming out their own shame; wandering stars, to whom is reserved the blackness of darkness for ever."

Jude 12-13

CHAPTER EIGHT

THE BLACKNESS OF DARKNESS FOREVER

here are many important things to be considered in the Word of God, but none so important as eternity. I hope you have trusted Jesus Christ as your personal Savior because the Lord Jesus says, *"I am the way, the truth, and the life: no man cometh unto the Father, but by me"* (John 14:6). He is the only way to heaven.

I remember the glad hour in my life when I asked the Lord to forgive my sin, and by faith I received Christ as my personal Savior. I have learned since my entry into God's family that I can always trust the Lord. He remains the same. He said, *"I change not."*

The book of Jude deals with a religious crowd, apostates. These are not strange-looking creatures with horns, perhaps green in color, having serpentlike faces. These are normal-looking people who have all the religious trappings that identify them with believers. The problem is that they have looked at revealed truth and turned from it. They look like Christians in many ways. They talk like Christians in many ways, but they have denied the Lord Jesus Christ.

As we continue our study in this book, I pray it will stir our hearts. The Bible says in verses twelve and thirteen of Jude,

> *These are spots in your feasts of charity, when they feast with you, feeding themselves without fear: clouds they are without water, carried about of winds; trees whose fruit withereth, without fruit, twice dead, plucked up by the roots; raging waves of the sea, foaming out their own shame; wandering stars, to whom is reserved the blackness of darkness for ever.*

God says that their end is the *"blackness of darkness for ever."*

There is a real heaven with a real street of gold and gates of pearl. When God beautifully describes heaven to us in the Bible,

> *Is it not amazing that darkness came into this world with a promise of light?*

He quickly moves to the Person of Jesus Christ. Revelation 22:4 says, *"And they shall see his face; and his name shall be in their foreheads."* There would be no heaven without Christ.

If you believe in a real heaven, then you should believe in a real hell. If heaven is a place where there is no need of the sun or the moon because the Son of God is the light, then remember that hell is a place with *"the blackness of darkness for ever."*

No one lives without dying. The Bible says in Hebrews 9:27, *"And as it is appointed unto men once to die, but after this the judgment."* For Christians, eternal life begins the moment the

Lord Jesus Christ comes to live in them. Because all people will be in eternity in either heaven or hell, our hearts should be stirred because of those who are going into that *"blackness of darkness for ever."*

THE DARKNESS OF THIS WORLD

To help us understand that darkness exists, God tells us that we get a taste of it in this world. There is a kingdom of light in the world, and there is a kingdom of darkness. Our Lord Jesus Christ is the King of Glory and the King of the kingdom of light. The Devil is the prince of darkness and the leader of the kingdom of darkness.

The Bible says in Ephesians 6:10-12,

> *Finally, my brethren, be strong in the Lord, and in the power of his might. Put on the whole armour of God, that ye may be able to stand against the wiles of the devil. For we wrestle not against flesh and blood, but against principalities, against powers, against the rulers of the darkness of this world, against spiritual wickedness in high places.*

Every word in the Bible is significant. There is *"the blackness of darkness forever"* in the world to come for those who live and die without Christ.

There is darkness in this present world. This world was introduced to darkness in Genesis chapter three. There was nothing but light until then because God had moved upon the face of the deep. God had spoken the world into existence. God said, *"Let there be light."* There was nothing but that bright light, a kingdom of light, until there was rebellion in heaven and the prince of darkness came to this earth.

Satan channeled his message through a serpent to Adam and Eve. As the Devil spoke to them, he made a revealing statement. The Bible says in Genesis 3:1-5,

> *Now the serpent was more subtil than any beast of the field which the LORD God had made. And he said unto the woman, Yea, hath God said, Ye shall not eat of every tree of the garden? And the woman said unto the serpent, We may eat of the fruit of the trees of the garden: but of the fruit of the tree which is in the midst of the garden, God hath said, Ye shall not eat of it, neither shall ye touch it, lest ye die. And the serpent said unto the woman, Ye shall not surely die: for God doth know that in the day ye eat thereof, then your eyes shall be opened, and ye shall be as gods, knowing good and evil.*

Darkness is never more dangerous than when it comes packaged as light.

Is it not amazing that darkness came into this world with a promise of light? Satan is the master deceiver! Sin entered into the bloodstream of all humanity through our first parents, Adam and Eve. The world was plunged into darkness. There has never been born since that time any man who was not a sinner except the God-Man, the Lord Jesus Christ who was born of a virgin.

We live in a world of darkness. We were plunged into this world of darkness with a promise of light. The Devil still makes the same promise. He makes the promise that his way is a better way. Darkness is never more dangerous than when it comes packaged as light.

The worst thing in your city is not some bar. The worst thing is not some crack house, though these are awful places. The worst thing is not some house of ill repute where people sell their flesh for money. The worst thing is a church where people appear to tell the truth but tell a lie. People believe the lies they hear and die and go to hell–*"the blackness of darkness for ever."*

Can you think of anything more pitiful than someone looking for hope and help, coming to a church building and hearing a man deny the truth of the Word of God? Can you think of anything worse than someone taking their children into a church building that should be lifting up Jesus Christ and finding that they are denying the truth? The worst thing in this world is a place that claims to be a beacon of light but is a house of darkness.

> *The worst thing in your city is not some bar. The worst thing is not some crack house, though these are awful places. The worst thing is not some house of ill repute where people sell their flesh for money. The worst thing is a church where people appear to tell the truth but tell a lie.*

This world is plagued with darkness. The longer I live, the darker it seems to get. Christian people must be stirred up about it.

> *There is nothing as dangerous as false religion. People with hungry, hurting hearts reach out for help and receive nothing but deception.*

Someone gave me an article recently about a particular bill to be passed that would require employers to give minority rights to homosexuals. In this same article there was a statement attributed to a well-known gay activist. This practicing homosexual stated that "someday all laws banning homosexual activity will be revoked. Instead of legislation prohibiting homosexuality, laws will be passed which engenders love between men. All the churches that condemn us will be closed. Our only gods are handsome young men."

In an article he wrote for the *Gay Community News* dated February 15, 1987, he said,

> We shall seduce your sons, emblems of your feeble masculinity, emblems of your shallow dreams and vulgar lies. We shall seduce them in your schools, in your dormitories, in your gymnasiums, in your locker rooms, in your sports arenas, in your seminaries, in your youth groups, in your movie theater bathrooms, in your army bunkhouses, in your truck stops, in your all-male clubs, in your houses of Congress, wherever men are with men together, we shall seduce your sons. Your sons shall become what

we want them to become at our bidding. They will be re-cast in our image. They will come to crave and adore us.

This kind of rhetoric may not be used often, but if you think it is nonsensical and irrational to be concerned about such a thing, then why do you insist on your husband going into a public restroom with your sons? Why do you insist on your wife going into a public restroom with your daughters? You know this is the kind of dark world in which we are living. It is unfortunate, sad, heartbreaking, and hard to explain to children, but it is true. We live in a dark world.

Of course, the homosexual community is not synonymous with apostates, but this is a terrible indication of how very wicked our world has become. The truth of God's Word must be heard throughout our land.

THE DECEPTION OF THESE APOSTATES

These apostates are not who they say they are. The Bible says in Jude 12, *"These are spots in your feasts of charity, when they feast with you, feeding themselves without fear...."* These spots mentioned here are dangerous places. As Jude speaks of love, feasts of charity, and celebrations of love, he says that these are like places of wreckage and danger. These are like rocks in uncharted water that cause shipwreck, while they claim to be guides.

He continues, *"...clouds they are without water, carried about of winds...."* They are like clouds appearing with a promise of rain but giving no rain. *"...trees whose fruit withereth, without fruit, twice dead, plucked up by the roots...."* They are as trees that appear to bear fruit, but they have no fruit and no root. They make promises but are twice dead. They are not what they say they are.

"Raging waves of the sea, foaming out their own shame."

We are dealing with two major problems. The first one is that many Christian people do not know what they believe. The second is that many who know what they believe do not tell what they know.

They boldly express their ideas and opinions, proclaiming their own shame.

The Bible says in verse thirteen that they are *"wandering stars."* They are falling stars, bright and beautiful, but they last only for a moment. Then they are nothing more than ashes. They are not what they say they are.

This is a day and hour when many who make use of the television and radio claim to be Christians, but they are anything but Christians. Some of them carry Bibles which they do not believe. They hold a Bible, yet they deny the Bible. They talk about Jesus but do not know the Lord Jesus or love Him.

You may ask, "Who are you to judge?" I do not have to be a judge. I only have to know the truth. When I know the truth and they do not speak the truth, I know that what they are speaking is not truth.

There is nothing as dangerous as false religion. People with hungry, hurting hearts reach out for help and receive nothing but deception. We should boldly declare the truth and stand up for what the Bible teaches. Let us proclaim the truth in love.

We are dealing with two major problems. The first one is that many Christian people do not know what they believe. The second is that many who know what they believe do not tell what they know.

Do not be ashamed. Be kind, but be a Christian and stand up for what you believe. Speak boldly for the Lord.

THE DOOM OF THESE PEOPLE

The Bible says that they are going into *"the blackness of darkness for ever."* The Bible says in Jude 4,

> *For there are certain men crept in unawares, who were before of old ordained to this condemnation, ungodly men, turning the grace of our God into lasciviousness, and denying the only Lord God, and our Lord Jesus Christ.*

The Lord provides examples in verses five, six, and seven. Then God declares in verses eight through eleven, *"Likewise also these...."* He speaks of these people, these apostates and these religious leaders, who have crept in unawares.

> *...these filthy dreamers defile the flesh, despise dominion, and speak evil of dignities. Yet Michael the archangel, when contending with the devil he disputed about the body of Moses, durst not bring against him a railing accusation, but said, The Lord rebuke thee. But these speak evil of those things which they know not: but what they know naturally, as brute beasts, in*

those things they corrupt themselves. Woe unto them! for they have gone in the way of Cain, and ran greedily after the error of Balaam for reward, and perished in the gainsaying of Core.

The Bible says that they are doomed. Their doom is *"the blackness of darkness for ever."* It is certainly not popular to preach on hell. It is popular to preach on love, but it is loving to tell people there is a hell.

Hell is real. The reason Christ came to die on the cross was to save people from hell. The logic of the gospel is that men need good news. Why do they need good news? The bad news is that if people die in their sin, they are going into the blackness of darkness forever.

Over a century ago, there lived a preacher by the name of Elbert Munsey. The Knoxville, Tennessee, paper called him the most eloquent man in the south. Almost all his preaching was on the subject of hell. He went up and down the land preaching on hell. Mr. Munsey died in 1877 in Jonesboro, Tennessee; he was forty-four years old. Many of his messages on the subject of hell were placed in book form.

In one of his messages, entitled "Eternal Retribution," Mr. Munsey said that he was sitting in his study, musing over the Word of God, praying, and asking God to help him prepare a message. He was thinking about hell, and he began to pen some thoughts about hell. These words were written 120 years ago,

> Hell may be a gloomy, desolate, and barren world whose rocks and mountains are tumbled into anarchy, but there are no blessed flowers, nodding trees, dewy vales, grassy slopes, and running streams. There are no homes, no

churches, no preaching, no morality, no religion, no friendships, and no God. Then the best hell we can promise is a world of ugly ruins shrouded in night's blackest darkness where no one of the damned has a friend. It is a place filled with cursings and strifes, where are ranks and sexes herded in one promiscuous mob with the foulest demons and where every stinking cave is inhabited with fiend, gnashing ghosts, and on whose black crags ravens of despair sit and croak and where God's eternal justice plies His burning whip and remorse lays on with fiery thongs. The flashes of whips and thongs are their only light, wild without end, darkness forever. It may be some huge cavern, howling out the center of some blasted, shattered, and God-cursed planet in which the poison and the stench of ages have gathered and condensing is still on the walls, dimly lit by sulphuric torches held by grimacing and howling fiends whose sickly flickerings render the darkness in all the winding pits, chasms, and corridors but blacker. Occasional blue flames break through the fissures overhead, lick along the arches and bolts of thunder, crash through the grottos in which lost men and fallen angels may be driven from the Judgment Seat. The ponderous gates close and lock behind them, the key fastened to the girdle of God and the divine omnipotent installed as perpetual signal to guard the way in this darkness forever. It may be an unquenchable lake of fire and brimstone, bubbles dancing on every wave and bursting fumes and smoke threaded with serpent flames in whose ascending volumes everlasting lightning flash and cross the darkness forever.

Just as real as your home town is real, hell is a real place. God says that there are those who are going into *"the blackness of darkness for ever."*

Remember always that God's work is greater than Satan's work. Satan's work can be undone, but God's work of saving lost souls can never be undone.

The Deliverance in Jesus Christ

We have considered the darkness of this world, the doom of these apostates, and the deception of these people. Let us consider the deliverance we have in Jesus Christ.

Once a child of darkness, now I am a child of light. The Bible says in John 1:4-5, *"In him was life; and the life was the light of men. And the light shineth in darkness; and the darkness comprehended it not."* The darkness of this world could not consume the light of Jesus Christ. It could not understand all of this light. This light is the true Light.

The Bible says in John 1:9, *"That was the true Light, which lighteth every man that cometh into the world."* That true Light is Jesus Christ. The Bible says in I Peter 2:9,

> *But ye are a chosen generation, a royal priesthood, an holy nation, a peculiar people; that ye should shew forth the praises of him who*

hath called you out of darkness into his marvellous light.

I was doomed and damned, and I was headed for darkness with no hope of heaven. The best I could have done was to live a meaningless life.

Recently a man and his wife moved to our city. They moved because the man said one day to his wife, "I don't want to turn out like everyone else I know has turned out. So what if we live in a beautiful home? So what if we drive a nice car? So what if we have two lovely children? There is more to life than this. We need the Lord and a church that will instruct us on how to live."

There is a Savior who will give us purpose, meaning, and fulfillment. He can deliver us from the kingdom of darkness to light. His name is Jesus Christ. He has forgiven my sin, delivered me from darkness, and brought me into His glorious light. We must trust Him, live for Him, and tell others about Him. Remember always that God's work is greater than Satan's work. Satan's work can be undone, but God's work of saving lost souls can never be undone. Let us proclaim the saving message of Jesus Christ.

*"And Enoch also, the
seventh from Adam,
prophesied of these, saying,
Behold, the Lord cometh
with ten thousands of his
saints, To execute judgment
upon all, and to convince
all that are ungodly among
them of all their ungodly
deeds which they have
ungodly committed, and of
all their hard speeches
which ungodly sinners
have spoken against him."*

Jude 14-15

CHAPTER
NINE

THE LORD IS COMING

 n our study of Jude, we come now to the great theme of the Second Coming of Jesus Christ. After salvation, there is nothing to compare with the consideration given to the coming again of Jesus Christ.

Remember that the book of Jude deals with apostates, religious people who look at revealed truth and turn from it. Sometimes we wonder how long they will go on. Will it last forever–their lies and their deception? Will wrong continue without ever being made right? With this thought in mind, the Bible says in Jude 14-15,

> *And Enoch also, the seventh from Adam, prophesied of these, saying, Behold, the Lord cometh with ten thousands of his saints, to execute judgment upon all, and to convince all that are ungodly among them of all their ungodly deeds which they have ungodly committed, and of all their hard speeches which ungodly sinners have spoken against him.*

The Bible says that *"the Lord cometh."* Oh, how we need to be stirred! We know what to do; we need to get busy doing it! We need to be motivated and stirred to live for our Lord.

The pressing need in the work of God is the need for revival. A revival is a new beginning of obedience to God. When we speak of revival, we are speaking about a revival of the church. We must talk about where it starts–it starts with revival of the individual heart. My heart needs to be revived, and your heart needs to be revived. Revival will be preceded by the preaching of the Second Coming of Jesus Christ.

The Bible says in II Peter 3:1-10,

> *This second epistle, beloved, I now write unto you; in both which I stir up your pure minds by way of remembrance: that ye may be mindful of the words which were spoken before by the holy prophets, and of the commandment of us the apostles of the Lord and Saviour: knowing this first, that there shall come in the last days scoffers, walking after their own lusts, and saying, Where is the promise of his coming? for since the fathers fell asleep, all things continue as they were from the beginning of the creation. For this they willingly are ignorant of, that by the word of God the heavens were of old, and the earth standing out of the water and in the water: whereby the world that then was, being overflowed with water, perished: but the heavens and the earth, which are now, by the same word are kept in store, reserved unto fire against the day of judgment and perdition of ungodly men. But, beloved, be not ignorant of this one thing, that one day is with the Lord as a thousand*

years, and a thousand years as one day. The Lord is not slack concerning his promise, as some men count slackness; but is longsuffering to us-ward, not willing that any should perish, but that all should come to repentance. But the day of the Lord will come as a thief in the night; in the which the heavens shall pass away with a great noise, and the elements shall melt with fervent heat, the earth also and the works that are therein shall be burned up.

Think of it! *"The Lord is not slack concerning his promise."* In this passage, he speaks of one promise, the singular promise of His return. The Lord is not slack concerning any of His promises, plural. They are all true, but here God speaks of one promise. He makes much of this one promise, the promise of the coming of our Lord Jesus Christ.

The Bible says He is coming again. This particular doctrine is given to us in the book of Jude. As it becomes active in our lives, the Lord will use it to stir our hearts.

THE PROPHECY CONCERNING HIS COMING

"And Enoch also, the seventh from Adam, prophesied of these, saying, Behold, the Lord cometh."

Some people make quite a fuss concerning this comment about Enoch, wondering why the human instrument God used to pen this book would include such a statement. Remember that all Scripture is given by inspiration of God. If God saw fit to include in His Word any statement or quotation from something or someone, then inspiration is fulfilled in the fact that it is recorded just as God intended for it to be recorded.

We know that such a man named Enoch lived, though the Bible does not tell us in the Old Testament of his prophecy. The Bible says that this man prophesied concerning the coming of the Lord.

When we see the word *"prophecy,"* we think of things foretold, things yet to take place. When speaking of a prophet in the Bible, we are speaking of someone who has been given revelation from God to "foretell" things. The prophet is also someone who is engaged in "forth telling." So there is "foretelling" and "forth telling." Foretelling is revealing things that are yet to take place, and forth telling is declaring with authority the message of God.

Near the end of the first century, the Lord had given all the written revelation He would give. The Bible is complete; God is not adding any written revelation to the Bible. A tremendous injustice has also been done by people saying, "This is what a certain Scripture means to me." I remind you that the Bible is not to be interpreted by what it means to individuals. The Bible is to be interpreted in its context. It may be applied in hundreds of ways, but there is one interpretation of Scripture.

There are two aspects of the Lord's return that are taught in the Bible. The first is the Rapture of the church, and the second is Christ's revelation, His coming in judgment. The Rapture of the church will take place first. This passage in the book of Jude has to do with the revelation of Jesus Christ, His coming in judgment. In John chapter fourteen, the Bible speaks of the Rapture when the Lord Jesus comes for His own. The Bible says in John 14:1-6,

> *Let not your heart be troubled: ye believe in*
> *God, believe also in me. In my Father's house*

are many mansions: if it were not so, I would have told you. I go to prepare a place for you. And if I go and prepare a place for you, I will come again, and receive you unto myself; that where I am, there ye may be also. And whither I go ye know, and the way ye know. Thomas saith unto him, Lord, we know not whither thou goest; and how can we know the way? Jesus saith unto him, I am the way, the truth, and the life: no man cometh unto the Father, but by me.

Notice the expression our Lord gives us in the third verse of John chapter fourteen, *"I will come again."* The Bible teaches that the Lord Jesus Christ is coming for His church before the Tribulation begins. The church will not go through the Tribulation.

One of the great Old Testament pictures of a New Testament truth is found in the man Enoch. He walked with God, and God took him before the flood. We believe in the pretribulational, premillennial view of the Second Coming of Christ because this is what we find in the Bible. The Lord is coming for His church before the Tribulation. We call ourselves premillennialists because we know that Jesus Christ must come before we will have the thousand years of peace upon this earth. The Lord Jesus Christ is coming to reign.

Foretelling is revealing things that are yet to take place, and forth telling is declaring with authority the message of God.

All of this may sound a bit oversimplified, but there are people who read this who know very little about the coming of

135

Christ. They have heard about His birth, His coming to earth, but they have heard very little about His coming again.

In the book of Acts, the Bible records that our Lord was taken up to heaven from the Mount of Olives. As His disciples stood by, He ascended up into heaven. The Bible says in Acts 1:10-11,

> *And while they looked stedfastly toward heaven as he went up, behold, two men stood by them in white apparel; which also said, Ye men of Galilee, why stand ye gazing up into heaven? this same Jesus, which is taken up from you into heaven, shall so come in like manner as ye have seen him go into heaven.*

This same Jesus is coming again. Prophecy concerning our Lord's Second Coming is clearly established in the Word of God. The Bible says in Jude 14, *"And Enoch also, the seventh from Adam, prophesied of these."*

Let us look at Enoch in the book of Genesis. He was the seventh from Adam. The Bible says in Genesis 5:1-3,

> *This is the book of the generations of Adam. In the day that God created man, in the likeness of God made he him; male and female created he them; and blessed them, and called their name Adam, in the day when they were created. And Adam lived an hundred and thirty years, and begat a son in his own likeness, after his image; and called his name Seth.*

This was the first generation. Notice in verse six, *"And Seth lived an hundred and five years, and begat Enos."* Then in verse nine the Bible says, *"And Enos lived ninety years, and begat Cainan."* Verse twelve says, *"And Cainan lived seventy years, and*

begat Mahalaleel." Notice verse fifteen, *"And Mahalaleel lived sixty and five years, and begat Jared."* Verse eighteen says, *"And Jared lived an hundred sixty and two years, and he begat Enoch."* The Bible says in verses twenty-one through twenty-four,

> *And Enoch lived sixty and five years, and begat Methuselah: and Enoch walked with God after he begat Methuselah three hundred years, and begat sons and daughters: and all the days of Enoch were three hundred sixty and five years: and Enoch walked with God: and he was not; for God took him.*

In the fourteenth verse of Jude, God tells us about Enoch and the prophecy that God gave him to declare. When we come to this seventh generation, Enoch represents the generation that did not die. Six generations had lived and died. Here is a beautiful type of the generation that lives and does not die. There is going to be a generation alive when Jesus Christ comes again. From among that generation the saved will be called out to be with Him.

The Bible says that Enoch had a son named Methuselah. Methuselah's name means, "When I die, God will send it." We are speaking of judgment. If you ask children to find the oldest person in the Bible, they will find the answer to be Methuselah. Is it not interesting to you that the Bible says in II Peter 3:9 that the Lord is *"not willing that any should perish, but that all should come to repentance"*? Our Lord does not want anyone to die and go to hell. In Genesis chapter five, the Lord told Enoch to name his son Methuselah. This meant that when it came time for Methuselah to die, the judgment of God would come. He lived longer than any other man who ever lived on earth, staying the hand of God's judgment 969 years. Then the judgment of God came. Every year Methuselah lived was a year closer to the

> *The Bible is to be interpreted in its context. It may be applied in hundreds of ways, but there is one interpretation of Scripture.*

coming of God's judgment–a year of mercy.

When our Lord, through divine inspiration, gives us this word in the book of Jude, declaring the prophecy of Enoch, He also wants to call our attention to this fifth chapter of Genesis and remind us that He is a patient God, a longsuffering God, a God of grace and mercy, and He is extending that mercy to all mankind. When Methuselah died, judgment fell. The day of judgment will come, just as surely as it came in Methuselah's day.

THE PROGRAM OF HIS COMING

The Bible says, *"And Enoch also, the seventh from Adam, prophesied of these, saying, Behold, the Lord cometh with ten thousands of his saints."* When we speak of the Rapture of the church, we mean by this that our Lord is coming *for* His saints. When we speak of the revelation of our Lord, we mean that the Lord is coming *with* His saints.

Notice the key verse of the book of Revelation, Revelation 1:19, *"Write the things which thou hast seen, and the things which are, and the things which shall be hereafter."* There are three divisions in the book of the Revelation. The first chapter deals with things that are past. Chapters two and three deal with things that are present, the church age. As we come to the opening of the fourth chapter, the church is gone–this begins the division of things to come, extending from chapters four through twenty-two.

God allows us to look into heaven in chapters four and five. When we come to chapters six through nineteen, we no longer find the church on earth. We are dealing with the period referred to as the Tribulation period on the earth.

Speaking of our Lord's return, the Bible says in Revelation 1:7, *"Behold, he cometh with clouds; and every eye shall see him, and they also which pierced him: and all kindreds of the earth shall wail because of him. Even so, Amen."* Here our Lord deals with both parts of His return.

The Rapture of the church is a secret coming, as a thief in the night. When the trumpet sounds in the Rapture, only the saved will hear it. God's Word says that the dead in Christ shall rise first.

When the Rapture takes place, a person could walk through a cemetery and not notice anything different because the body that is raised from the dead will be like the resurrected body of Jesus Christ. The molecular structure of the Christian's glorified body is not like the body that we have today. The structure of our Lord's resurrected body enabled Him to walk through solid walls and doors. The resurrected body will pass through the earth without disturbing the dust or a blade of grass. It will be a different body.

Every saved person on the earth will be missing, and all the children throughout the world who are under the time of their personal accountability to God will be taken also. The Lord is coming again. He will come to rapture the church in a moment, in the twinkling of an eye. We will be gone. Then the earth will enter the Tribulation period. This will last for seven years. The last three and a half years will be the Great Tribulation. At the end of that Tribulation, the Lord is coming with ten thousands of His saints to execute judgment upon this unbelieving world.

In Revelation 19:9, the Bible speaks of the marriage supper of the Lamb. There will be two feasts, one with the Lord Jesus at the marriage of the Lamb, and the other as beasts feed on the dead bodies of the slain of the earth. The Bible says in Revelation 19:11-16,

> *And I saw heaven opened, and behold a white horse; and he that sat upon him was called Faithful and True, and in righteousness he doth judge and make war. His eyes were as a flame of fire, and on his head were many crowns; and he had a name written that no man knew, but he himself. And he was clothed with a vesture dipped in blood: and his name is called The Word of God. And the armies which were in heaven followed him upon white horses, clothed in fine linen, white and clean. And out of his mouth goeth a sharp sword, that with it he should smite the nations: and he shall rule them with a rod of iron: and he treadeth the winepress of fierceness and wrath of Almighty God. And he hath on his vesture and on his thigh a name written, KING OF KINGS, AND LORD OF LORDS.*

This is the revelation of Jesus Christ when He comes with ten thousands of His saints. He is coming again!

There is no sign for our Lord's return for His own. When we read of these signs in the Bible, it is speaking of His revelation at the end of the Tribulation period. Revelation chapter six deals with the first four seals and the famous horsemen. Compare this chapter with the Olivet Discourse given by Jesus Christ in

Matthew 24 as our Lord answered His disciples in verses four through seven, *"Take heed that no man deceive you. For many shall come in my name, saying, I am Christ; and shall deceive many."* This is the white horse. *"And ye shall hear of wars and rumours of wars: see that ye be not troubled: for all these things must come to pass, but the end is not yet."* This is the red horse. *"For nation shall rise against nation, and kingdom against kingdom: and there shall be famines...."* This is the black horse. *"...and pestilences, and earthquakes, in divers places."* This is the pale horse of death. We find the same thing in the Olivet Discourse in Matthew 24 that we find in Revelation 6 during the Tribulation period.

Christ will come for His church. Seven years later, at the revelation of Jesus Christ, He will come with His church. I am going up when He comes *for* His church, and I am coming back when He comes *with* His church. This is God's program. Our hope is

When our Lord, through divine inspiration, gives us this word in the book of Jude, declaring the prophecy of Enoch, He also wants to call our attention to this fifth chapter of Genesis and remind us that He is a patient God, a longsuffering God, a God of grace and mercy, and He is extending that mercy to all mankind.

not in the Second Coming of Christ, but rather in the Christ of the Second Coming.

THE PURPOSE OF HIS COMING

The purpose of the Rapture is to receive the bride. The purpose of the revelation seven years later is for judgment. The Bible says in Jude 15,

> *To execute judgment upon all, and to convince all that are ungodly among them of all their ungodly deeds which they have ungodly committed, and of all their hard speeches which ungodly sinners have spoken against him.*

Normally, when we think about the ungodly, we think about some vile, blasphemous kind of person. Perhaps a person like Madelyn Murray O'Hare who waged a campaign that was anti-God, anti-Christ, anti-Bible, anti-Christian, and anti-church. The apostates revealed to us in the book of Jude are not necessarily boisterous, loud God-defiers and God-deniers. The ungodly refusing submission to the Lord Jesus Christ are the winsome, the beautiful, the articulate, and the religious without Christ. Hundreds and thousands of them state their ideas and purposes all around the world. All of them embody an anti-Christ philosophy.

The prefix *anti-* means "against or instead of." This word *antichrist* can be used in three ways. First, it can mean any doctrine or teaching that is against Christ or instead of Christ. A man will go to hell believing in something other than Christ. It is not a matter of standing against Christ; if you give a man something instead of Christ, he will go to hell believing it.

Second, the word can be used for anyone who embodies a doctrine that is instead of or against Christ. There are many antichrists who are proponents of religious ways that are substitutes for Christ.

Third, the word is used for the Antichrist who shall make his appearance when the church is gone.

God is coming to judge this world. How long will it continue before God says, "Enough"? When the church of the living God is gone from the earth and the restraining work of the Holy Spirit is removed for seven years, men will say, "I've got my turn now without God. We'll show everyone what can be done without Christ and without the Bible." It will be a vile, wicked world where hell has been opened and evil spirits set loose. It will be a religious world. The earth will become a bloodbath. The wicked world will have its last fling, thinking they had their way. They will be ready to shake their fists in the face of God when suddenly heaven will open and the Lord God Almighty will come in His revelation to execute judgment. This is the purpose of His Second Coming.

> *Our hope is not in the Second Coming of Christ, but rather in the Christ of the Second Coming.*

The Lord Jesus is coming again! Be sure that you are a Christian. Trust in Christ and Christ alone for your soul's salvation and live each day looking for and loving His appearing.

"These are murmurers, complainers, walking after their own lusts; and their mouth speaketh great swelling words, having men's persons in admiration because of advantage. But, beloved, remember ye the words which were spoken before of the apostles of our Lord Jesus Christ; How that they told you there should be mockers in the last time, who should walk after their own ungodly lusts. These be they who separate themselves, sensual, having not the Spirit."

Jude 16-19

CHAPTER TEN

THEY DO NOT HAVE
THE HOLY SPIRIT

ur most dangerous enemies are the enemies who appear as friends. May God give us discernment to know the real enemies of the cross of Christ and the work of the Lord Jesus.

In this passage, we notice something very definite about these people. The Bible says in verses sixteen through nineteen,

> These are murmurers, complainers, walking after their own lusts; and their mouth speaketh great swelling words, having men's persons in admiration because of advantage. But, beloved, remember ye the words which were spoken before of the apostles of our Lord Jesus Christ; How that they told you there should be mockers in the last time, who should walk after their own ungodly lusts. These be they who separate themselves, sensual, having not the Spirit.

Notice the words *"having not the Spirit."* With this in mind, let us consider I John chapter four. The Bible says in verse one,

"Beloved, believe not every spirit, but try the spirits whether they are of God: because many false prophets are gone out into the world."

The Bible says in Jude 19 that they have *"not the Spirit,"* speaking of the Holy Spirit. In I John chapter four the Bible says, *"Believe not every spirit, but try the spirits...."* The word here, *"spirits,"* is plural. *"...whether they are of God."* There are many spirits in this world, but there is only one Holy Spirit. The question we must face is whether or not we are indwelt by the Holy Spirit. Are you sure that the Holy Spirit lives in you? At the moment of salvation the Holy Spirit comes to indwell every believer forever.

The things that characterize the lives of these apostates are sometimes shocking. The Bible says very plainly that, when God looks inside the hearts of these apostates, they do not have the Spirit–the Holy Spirit.

In the fifteenth verse of Jude the Bible says,

> *To execute judgment upon all, and to convince all that are ungodly among them of all their ungodly deeds which they have ungodly committed, and of all their hard speeches which ungodly sinners have spoken against him.*

They speak against Jesus Christ. The direction of all their hard speeches is against Jesus Christ. Some people may have the idea that what these apostates speak is against someone who stands for Christ or against some church that takes a stand for Christ, but the Bible says that everything they are doing is against Christ.

The Bible says in the sixteenth verse, *"These are murmurers, complainers, walking after their own lusts; and their mouth*

speaketh great swelling words, having men's persons in admiration because of advantage." They murmur and complain, and they mock the truth, *"having men's persons in admiration because of advantage."* These apostates are not motivated by truth but rather by the approval of men.

The faithful pastor must love people and must love to be around people, but he has a message to preach and his God to please. Whether people accept it or not, if God wants the people to hear it, then the preacher should preach it.

> *These apostates are not motivated by truth but rather by the approval of men.*

I was talking to a young man recently about his high school experience. He went to a special high school. I said, "Did you graduate?" He said, "Yes, I have a diploma." I said, "No, did you graduate?" He said, "Well, I have a diploma. I did not graduate, but I have a diploma." I said, "Well, that means you graduated." He said, "No, they let me walk across the stage, and they put a diploma in my hand, but I don't call it graduating." I said, "What do you mean?" He said, "I was robbed. I was cheated." I said, "What do you mean by that?" He replied, "Some of the subject matter I just couldn't get, so they just passed me anyway. They thought they were doing me a favor by letting me slide, but I realize now as a young adult with what I am expected to know and expected to be able to do that they didn't help me. They hurt me."

As I thought about what he said, I realized the same truth applies to the church. If the preacher simply pats you on the back and tells you everything you want to hear and does not preach the truth to you, if he will not stand up and tell you what God wants you to hear, he is not helping you. He is hurting you.

Stay with the truth! Every word of the Bible is the Word of God. Hell is real. I do not enjoy talking to people about hell. I do not enjoy preaching on hell, but nevertheless hell is a real place. If I said to you that hell is not a real place, I would be calling Jesus Christ a liar because He said in Luke 16:23-24,

> *And in hell he lift up his eyes, being in torments, and seeth Abraham afar off, and Lazarus in his bosom. And he cried and said, Father Abraham, have mercy on me, and send Lazarus, that he may dip the tip of his finger in water, and cool my tongue; for I am tormented in this flame.*

This is what the Lord Jesus said. Hell is a real place.

Heaven is also a real place, not a state of mind. The only way to heaven is by trusting in Jesus Christ and Him alone for salvation. The Christian life is a holy life. Every Christian should be a Spirit-filled Christian. We must not say what we say because we think it will please people. We must say what we say because we know that preaching and teaching the truth pleases God.

We have been warned. The Bible says in verse eighteen, *"How that they told you there should be mockers in the last time, who should walk after their own ungodly lusts."* Remember the word *"mockers."* Take warning here!

God concludes with this group before He turns our attention toward those who know and love Him. He lists definite things about these apostates in verse nineteen.

THEY SEPARATE THEMSELVES

Jude 19 says, *"These be they who separate themselves."* This group says that we separate ourselves, but that is not what the Bible says. The Bible says, *"They separate themselves."*

Those of us who, by faith, stand where God's Word stands realize that there are times when people do not continue to stand where they once stood. By refusing to disobey the Lord and the clear commands of His Word, we are often accused of being stubborn, or even pharasaical. The truth of the matter is, if we, as the apostle Paul said to Timothy, *"continue"* in the things we have learned, there are those who separate from us because they do not *"continue."*

My wife and I started out in a denomination and then became independent Baptists by conviction.

> *The faithful pastor must love people and must love to be around people, but he has a message to preach and his God to please. Whether people accept it or not, if God wants the people to hear it, then the preacher should preach it.*

In reality, I felt that the group I was associated with had left us because we had not changed our position on Christ and His Word. There are those in life who *"separate themselves"* from us by their doctrine and deeds. Let us stay with the Bible and never waver.

Truth reveals division. Everything religious people believe is not true, and the truth of God's Word provides the standard for faith and practice. Those who do not believe the Bible to be without error have separated themselves from those who do.

THEY ARE SENSUAL

The Bible says in verse nineteen, *"These be they who separate themselves, sensual."* This word *"sensual"* has to do with all things that are natural. This has to do with living life not by faith but by the natural senses.

> *Every Christian should be a Spirit-filled Christian.*

The Bible says in I Corinthians 2:14, *"But the natural man receiveth not the things of the Spirit of God: for they are foolishness unto him: neither can he know them, because they are spiritually discerned."* Notice that *"the natural man"* does not receive them, and notice his response, *"They are foolishness unto him."* The matter of faith in God cannot be dealt with by those who have no faith in the only true God.

Sensual does not necessarily mean sexual, but it does mean a lack of faith in the true and living God. It is a life lived by the base things of this world.

The Christian must live the faith life. The Bible says that these apostates are *"sensual."*

THEY HAVE NOT THE SPIRIT

The Word of God describes these apostates as *"having not the Spirit."* They have never been born again.

They separate themselves. They are sensual. All of this behavior comes to pass because they have not the Spirit. They are religious, but they have never trusted Christ as their personal Savior. It is shocking to think of how many people who identify with churches and religion may be lost.

John the Baptist spoke to a group of religious people in Matthew 3:2-7, saying,

> *Repent ye: for the kingdom of heaven is at hand. For this is he that was spoken of by the prophet Esaias, saying, The voice of one crying in the wilderness, prepare ye the way of the Lord, make his paths straight. And the same John had his raiment of camel's hair, and a leathern girdle about his loins; and his meat was locusts and wild honey. Then went out to him Jerusalem, and all Judaea, and all the region round about Jordan, and were baptized of him in Jordan, confessing their sins. But when he saw many of the Pharisees and Sadducees come to his baptism, he said unto them, O generation of vipers, who hath warned you to flee from the wrath to come?*

We need more preachers like John the Baptist. People may say, "You are unkind. You are making people mad." But what do people need today? If a man is lost, dying, and going to hell without Christ, should we not speak in a way that might wake him up and get him to realize that he has never been born again before he dies and goes to hell forever?

The Bible says that these apostates separate themselves, are sensual, and have not the Holy Spirit. But what about those of us who know the Lord? Our separation should be *from* the world and *unto* the Lord. Our lives should not be marked by sensual living but by faith in God. When was the last time you trusted God for something?

> *It is shocking to think of how many people who identify with churches and religion may be lost.*

The Bible says that they have not the Spirit, but if we have truly been born into God's family, we are indwelt by the Holy Spirit. The Bible says in Romans 8:9, *"But ye are not in the flesh, but in the Spirit, if so be that the Spirit of God dwell in you. Now if any man have not the Spirit of Christ, he is none of his."*

These people are not indwelt by the Holy Spirit. Look at the difference in their lives. They look at revealed truth and turn from it while maintaining the appearance of truth. Their lives are sensual. They separate themselves.

We know the truth. We should live lives separated unto God. We should trust the Lord. Because we are indwelt by the Holy Spirit, we should seek the Holy Spirit's fullness and be bold for Jesus Christ. Can you imagine if someone living next door to me was starving to death, and I had a kitchen full of food and did not feed him? What would you think of me?

In Cape Coral, Florida, a lady found a thirteen-year-old girl and her three-year-old brother sleeping in her garage, eating out of her garbage. They had no home because they had been thrown out. They shared part of their story with this elderly lady after she caught them. They had been in her garage for three days. When she went to make a phone call for help, they disappeared.

Not far from this lady's house, they uncovered a place where the two had built some sort of cardboard dwelling. They had been sleeping in the bushes. It had gotten so cold that they had to come inside. How many people who have shelter and food would be willing to share their shelter and food with that little thirteen-year-old girl and her three-year-old brother? Everyone I know would help them.

As I heard this story, God pierced my heart with conviction and said, "So many are spiritually hungry and without the eternal shelter provided by the blood of Jesus Christ, but so few Christians are willing to do anything to change it."

It is not enough to talk about the identifying marks of the apostates. May the God who indwells us convict us and help us to do what we know we need to do for the lost and dying in our world. Most of us have said enough about what we do not do. Let us begin to show the love of Christ to the lost around us.

"But ye, beloved,
building up yourselves
on your most holy faith,
praying in the Holy Ghost,
Keep yourselves in the love
of God, looking for the
mercy of our Lord Jesus
Christ unto eternal life."

Jude 20-21

LIVING RIGHT IN A WRONG WORLD

 o far in our study of the book of Jude, we have been walking through the darkness. We have witnessed the beliefs and behavior of the apostates.

In verse twenty of this book we turn the spiritual corner and the Lord says, *"But ye."* He speaks to those of us who are His children. The Bible says in Jude 20-21,

> *But ye, beloved, building up yourselves on your most holy faith, praying in the Holy Ghost, Keep yourselves in the love of God, looking for the mercy of our Lord Jesus Christ unto eternal life.*

Notice the first two words in the twentieth verse, *"But ye."* One cannot read this passage without realizing that God wants our attention. Does He have your attention?

Perhaps you have heard the old farm story about the farmer who sold a mule to a neighboring farmer. He promised the farmer to whom he sold the mule that it was a good, hardworking mule. He said, "Once you tell the mule what to do, he will be glad to do it." The fellow who bought the mule had him out the next day trying to plow, but he could not get the mule to do a thing.

So the farmer went to the fellow who sold him the mule and said, "I need some help." The fellow who sold the mule walked over, picked up a fallen tree limb, and hit the mule in the head knocking him to the ground. He then whispered to the mule, "Now plow." The mule got up and started right off to pull the plow. The man said, "I forgot to tell you that you had to get the mule's attention first."

> *One cannot read this passage without realizing that God wants our attention. Does He have your attention?*

The Lord wants our attention. Turning from these apostates, He speaks to the genuine, Bible-believing Christians, saying, *"But ye."* We are called upon to live right in a wrong world.

There is a difference between the way a Christian lives and the way an unbeliever lives. Unbelievers think differently than believers think. They behave differently. The world should be able to look at someone who is a Christian and know from the way that person lives and speaks that he is a Christian.

If Christians would just be Christian, we would have the greatest revival in the history of our nation. We have gotten to the place where we talk about *good* Christians and *bad* Christians, *cold* Christians and *hot* Christians. We should just be able to say, "That person is a *Christian*"–with no adjectives. That should be enough.

I do not know where we got the idea that we are doing God a favor by doing our reasonable service. We think we are doing God a favor if we are faithful to church, but we are supposed to be there. People think that if they tithe their income they are doing God a favor. The Bible commands that Christians should tithe. The tenth belongs to God.

We are stealing from the Lord if we do not practice tithing as a conviction. We are not doing God a favor. It is part of the Christian life. We are not doing God a favor by reading God's Word and praying. We are commanded to do these things.

The world should be able to look at someone who is a Christian and know from the way that person lives and speaks that he is a Christian.

The Christian life is a life that honors Christ. The only hope in this world is found in Jesus Christ. The only way this world is ever going to see Christ is to see Him in the lives of Christians.

Through these words Jude penned under the inspiration of the Spirit of God, God has called our attention again and again to these apostates who say one thing but live another. They speak great, swelling words, but their hearts are just as black as the charred walls of hell.

THE CALL TO LIVE RIGHT

In the closing words of this letter, the Lord turns to His own, saying, *"But ye."* In a wrong world, we must live right.

God gave a warning to the children of Israel in the fifth chapter of Isaiah. It is tremendously appropriate for our day. The Bible says in verses twenty and twenty-one,

> *Woe unto them that call evil good, and good evil; that put darkness for light, and light for darkness; that put bitter for sweet, and sweet for bitter! Woe unto them that are wise in their own eyes, and prudent in their own sight!*

God says, "My people are doing evil and calling it good. My people are living in darkness and calling it light. These people speak of bitter things as being sweet."

We have moved from the violation of God's standards to the repudiation of God's standards to the popularization and glorification of evil. To violate the standard of God is to declare, "I know it is wrong, but I'm going to do it anyway." To repudiate it is to say, "That is not for me. I refuse to acknowledge that the standard even exists."

When our Lord Jesus brought His disciples before Him to instruct them how to live, He said in Matthew 5:13,

> *Ye are the salt of the earth: but if the salt have lost his savour, wherewith shall it be salted? it is thenceforth good for nothing, but to be cast out, and to be trodden under foot of men.*

The chemical makeup of salt is not destroyed, but salt becomes ineffective when it is contaminated with other things.

When looking at the contaminated salt, one finds the chemical elements that make it salt, but it has no power remaining because it has become infiltrated with other things.

The Lord Jesus said, "You are the salt, but if you lose your savour, if you get so contaminated with the world, you have no power." So many who profess to be Christians live just like the rest of the world, look like the world, go where the world goes, and speak like the world speaks. Something is dreadfully wrong with their walk with God.

In the closing words of this letter, the Lord turns to His own, saying, "But ye." In a wrong world, we must live right.

Take to heart the words of the Lord Jesus in John chapter seventeen, verses eleven through seventeen. This is the high priestly prayer that the Lord Jesus offered.

> *And now I am no more in the world, but these are in the world, and I come to thee. Holy Father, keep through thine own name those whom thou hast given me, that they may be one, as we are. While I was with them in the world, I kept them in thy name: those that thou gavest me I have kept, and none of them is lost, but the son of perdition; that the scripture might be fulfilled. And now come I to thee; and these things I speak in the world, that they might have my joy fulfilled in themselves. I have given them thy word; and the world hath hated them, because they are not of the world, even as I am not of the world. I pray not that thou shouldest take them out of the world, but that thou shouldest keep them from the evil.*

It is not God's will to remove us from the world. If He removes us, who is going to witness? The Bible says in II Corinthians 6:14-18, *"Be ye not unequally yoked together with unbelievers: for what fellowship hath righteousness with unrighteousness?..."*

"Fellowship" means "what we have in common." If a man disgraces the name of Jesus Christ, cares nothing for the Bible, cares nothing for the church, and is filthy in his conversation, what fellowship can a Christian have with someone like that? We must love the lost. We should win the lost, but this cannot be done by living like the lost. The Bible continues,

> *...and what communion hath light with darkness? And what concord hath Christ with Belial? or what part hath he that believeth with an infidel? And what agreement hath the temple of God with idols? for ye are the temple of the living God; as God hath said, I will dwell in them, and walk in them; and I will be their God, and they shall be my people. Wherefore come out from among them, and be ye separate, saith the Lord, and touch not the unclean thing; and I will receive you, and will be a Father unto you, and ye shall be my sons and daughters, saith the Lord Almighty.*

God says we should be separated. This is two-fold—separated *to* the Lord and *from* the world. Separation does not mean isolation. The Lord Jesus said He does not want us isolated; He does not want us removed but separate. There is a difference. We are not to stay out of the world; we are to keep the world out of us.

As the world gets worse and worse, the New Testament church will mean more and more to the children of God. This is a very dark world, and we must determine to live right and make a difference.

THE COST OF LIVING RIGHT

It costs something to live right. It costs the loss of personal freedom. I am not my own; I belong to Christ. The saddest thing I hear from some Christians is the expression, "It's my life!" Then for whom did Christ die?

If we belong to the Lord, we are to yield our personal freedom and say, "I want Thy will to be done."

God says we should be separated. . . separated to the Lord and from the world. Separation does not mean isolation.

Living right will cost us social standing. When working, we owe an hour's work for an hour's pay. If we have an opportunity on the lunch break to share the gospel with someone who is interested, we should do it. You should be a witness at work, but you will lose your testimony by not doing an hour's work for an hour's pay. Live the Christian life. Be on time. Show up for work. Identify strongly with the Lord Jesus Christ.

One of our dear church members wore a button about Christ to work. He was called into the office and the boss said, "Your button is offensive. This Jesus stuff must go! You will have to take the button off." He said kindly, "I am not going to do that unless you get the others to take their Budweiser beer shirts off and rock music shirts off." The boss said, "Keep your button."

It is all right to live for the Devil as far as the world is concerned, but it is not all right to live for God. Do you know why? Because we are living in a world so wrong that they call darkness light and light darkness.

THE COURSE FOR LIVING RIGHT

God has a direction for us to follow. We have been called to live right, and we must be willing to pay the price. The Lord tells us how to live right; God has a course for us to follow. If we are going to live right, we must follow the plan God has for us in His Word. Put these things from the book of Jude to work in your life.

BUILD YOURSELF UP

The Bible says in Jude 20, *"But ye, beloved, building up yourselves on your most holy faith."* The first thing He says to do is to build yourself up. We have the right Foundation, Jesus Christ; build on Him.

As Paul greeted the Ephesian elders in Acts chapter twenty, his heart was stirred. The Bible says in Acts 20:17-25,

> *And from Miletus he sent to Ephesus, and called the elders of the church. And when they were come to him, he said unto them, Ye know, from the first day that I came into Asia, after what manner I have been with you at all seasons, serving the Lord with all humility of mind, and with many tears, and temptations, which befell me by thelying*

in wait of the Jews: and how I kept back nothing that was profitable unto you, but have shewed you, and have taught you publickly, and from house to house, testifying both to the Jews, and also to the Greeks, repentance toward God, and faith toward our Lord Jesus Christ. And now, behold, I go bound in the spirit unto Jerusalem, not knowing the things that shall befall me there: save that the Holy Ghost witnesseth in every city, saying that bonds and afflictions abide me. But none of these things move me, neither count I my life dear unto myself, so that I might finish my course with joy, and the ministry, which I have received of the Lord Jesus, to testify the gospel of the grace of God. And now, behold, I know that ye all, among whom I have gone preaching the kingdom of God, shall see my face no more.

If you want to know how much you love someone, think of what it would be like to see that person no more.

Paul said, "I have ministered among you. I have preached the truth, but I go and you will see my face no more." The Bible continues in verse twenty-six, *"Wherefore I take you to record this day, that I am pure from the blood of all men."*

Then he declares in verses twenty-seven through thirty-two,

For I have not shunned to declare unto you all the counsel of God. Take heed therefore unto yourselves, and to all the flock, over the which the Holy Ghost hath made you overseers, to feed the church of God, which he hath purchased with his own blood. For I know this, that after my departing shall grievous wolves enter in among you, not

sparing the flock. Also of your own selves shall men arise, speaking perverse things, to draw away disciples after them. Therefore watch, and remember, that by the space of three years I ceased not to warn every one night and day with tears. And now, brethren, I commend you to God, and to the word of his grace, which is able to build you up, and to give you an inheritance among all them which are sanctified.

Notice that *"the word of his grace"* is able to build us up. It is God's Word that builds us up. God says in Jude verse twenty that we are to build ourselves up. Acts 20:32 says that we build ourselves up with the Word of God.

When I came to Christ, I did not know the difference between the Old Testament and the New Testament, and I could not quote one verse of Scripture from memory. The person who led me to Christ used John 3:16. I could not quote that verse, but I wanted to become a Christian.

In order to live right in this evil world, we must build ourselves up by reading God's Word.

PRAY IN THE HOLY GHOST

Notice what else He says in verse twenty, *"Praying in the Holy Ghost."*

"Praying in the Holy Ghost" simply means to walk with the Lord in obedience to Christ, to pray as we walk with the Lord in the light of His Word, to fellowship with Him, and to ask anything in His name believing He will grant it. This is the only way to pray. The Bible says in John 14:13, *"And whatsoever ye*

shall ask in my name, that will I do, that the Father may be glorified in the Son."

The Bible says in I John 1:5-7,

> *This then is the message which we have heard of him, and declare unto you, that God is light, and in him is no darkness at all. If we say that we have fellowship with him, and walk in darkness, we lie, and do not the truth: but if we walk in the light, as he is in the light, we have fellowship one with another, and the blood of Jesus Christ his Son cleanseth us from all sin.*

When we are walking with the Lord, walking in the Holy Spirit and praying in the Spirit in the name of the Lord, we are doing what God has called us to do. What about your prayer life? I am ashamed when I say "prayer life." I am ashamed of how strong we could be and how weak we are; of how much we could have from God and how little we do have. In this wicked world, we must walk with God seeking His power on our lives.

KEEP YOURSELF IN THE LOVE OF GOD

The Bible says in Jude 20, *"Keep yourselves in the love of God."* This does not mean trying to get God to love you. There is nothing we can do to make God love us. He already loves us. There is nothing we can do to make God stop loving us. We are loved with an *"everlasting love."*

This verse teaches us to obey the Lord and stay in the place of blessing. When children go out the door and the weather is cold, their mother will say, "Stay in the sunshine. Stay in the place where it is warm." God says, "Keep yourself in the love of

God." Be sure to keep your eyes on the Lord Jesus. Think always of His great compassion.

LOOK FOR THE LORD'S RETURN

Again, the Bible says in Jude 20, *"Looking for the mercy of our Lord Jesus Christ unto eternal life."* This speaks of our Lord's return. It will change our lives to live in the light of the Second Coming of Jesus Christ. If I really believe that the Lord could come today, it will change the way I live.

When I was just a boy, my mother, brother, and two sisters went on a short vacation without me. I promised that I would be home and have the house cleaned when they returned. My mother called me at a friend's house and told me that she had arrived home a day early. The dishes in the house were dirty, my clothes were dirty, and the bed was not made. The house was a disaster.

My mother came home a day early. She came home on the day I was going to clean the house. I had big plans. I was going to get things done, but I had other frivolous things to do before I got busy doing the important things.

The Lord Jesus is coming early. The Bible says in Luke 12:40, *"Be ye therefore ready also: for the Son of man cometh at an hour when ye think not."*

Do you have a desire to be what you should be in order to live right in a wrong world? You must build yourself up, pray in the Holy Ghost, keep yourself in the love of God, and look for the Lord to return. If we will do these things, we can live right in a world that is wrong.

*"And of some have
compassion,
making a difference:*
*And others save with fear,
pulling them out of the fire;
hating even the garment
spotted by the flesh."*

Jude 22-23

CHAPTER TWELVE

HAVE COMPASSION, MAKING A DIFFERENCE

n our desire as Christians to be Christlike, there is always a struggle between hating sin and loving sinners.

We live in a world of things that trouble us. It is possible to be angry and sin not. Anger becomes sin when it is out of control. There should be some things in the world we see that make us angry as Christians.

I appreciate receiving mail from people who say, "We are glad to know where you stand." I like to hear folks say, "We are glad that you still stand against what is wrong."

A huge part of loving is declaring what is evil. In our churches, one should hear sermons about the judgment of God, hell, sin, and the wickedness of abominable things.

As we travel through this book of Jude, we find the Lord dealing with this awful age of apostasy and the horrible things that it produces. When we come to the twentieth verse He says, *"But ye."* We are *in* the world but not *of* the world.

He charges us in verses twenty through twenty-two,

> *But ye, beloved, building up yourselves on your most holy faith, praying in the Holy Ghost, keep yourselves in the love of God, looking for the mercy of our Lord Jesus Christ unto eternal life. And of some have compassion, making a difference.*

We need compassion. The Word of God says in Psalm 126:5-6, *"They that sow in tears shall reap in joy. He that goeth forth and weepeth, bearing precious seed, shall doubtless come again with rejoicing, bringing his sheaves with him."*

The difference is made when people care. It is an easy thing to see who has compassion and who does not have compassion. Compassion is having the hurt of others in our hearts. The greatest example of compassion is the cross of Calvary where Jesus Christ bore the hurt of our sin debt in His heart.

THE COMMAND TO CARE

God says, *"Have compassion."* Be a loving, caring person.

The interesting thing about this particular expression is the context. In a time of apostasy, in a world that is getting worse and worse, God says that we are to *"have compassion."* We should be honest about the thing. Wicked things we hear people say and wicked things we see people do make them more difficult to love. The emphasis of this Scripture is that when people are so terribly hard to love because of their wickedness, that is when we need to love more than ever.

Compassion breaks down barriers like nothing else can. Many people have had their hard hearts broken because of someone's tears. Many people who have determined to do harm to someone have had their intentions changed by someone's compassion. It does make a difference. We are commanded to care.

The Bible says in I John 3:16-18,

> *Hereby perceive we the love of God, because he laid down his life for us: and we ought to lay down our lives for the brethren. But whoso hath this world's good, and seeth his brother have need, and shutteth up his bowels of compassion from him, how dwelleth the love of God in him? My little children, let us not love in word, neither in tongue; but in deed and in truth.*

It is wonderful to hear people say, "I love you." You can tell when people say, "I love you" whether or not they are saying it from a heart of love. God commands us to love *"in deed."*

We should go out of our way to show compassion to people. We are to live above what is considered normal, above what is ordinary.

Compassion is having the hurt of others in our hearts.

As I look back across my life, I am sure that my testimony is similar to many others. Caring people were the ones God used to make a difference in my life.

Compassion costs something. Having compassion will take us out of the ordinary routine. So many of us are bothered by the least "inconveniences," but caring, compassionate people go out of their way, making a difference in the lives of others.

Compassion is something we do, not simply something we talk about.

We should be troubled because we are not troubled. We should be concerned because of our lack of concern. We should be weeping because we do not weep. God gives us a command to care when He says, *"Have compassion."*

THE CRY OF THE WORLD

In the ninth chapter of Mark, our Lord had been on the Mount of Transfiguration with three of His disciples. As they came back down to the valley and met the other disciples, they were confronted by a religious group. A great controversy was brewing because a man had brought his son to the disciples for healing and the disciples could not heal him. When they could not heal him, the leaders who were against Christ were ridiculing His disciples because of their inability to help the man. The Bible says in Mark 9:14-21,

> *Compassion costs something. Having compassion will take us out of the ordinary routine.*

And when he came to his disciples, he saw a great multitude about them, and the scribes questioning with them. And straightway all the people, when they beheld him, were greatly amazed, and running to him saluted him. And he asked the scribes, What question ye with them? And one of the multitude answered and said, Master, I have brought unto thee my

son, which hath a dumb spirit; and wheresoever he taketh him, he teareth him: and he foameth, and gnasheth with his teeth, and pineth away: and I spake to thy disciples that they should cast him out; and they could not. He answereth him, and saith, O faithless generation, how long shall I be with you? how long shall I suffer you? bring him unto me. And they brought him unto him: and when he saw him, straightway the spirit tare him; and he fell on the ground, and wallowed foaming, And he asked his father, How long is it ago since this came unto him? And he said, Of a child.

The father had lived with this for all of this boy's life. In verse twenty-two, the man said to Christ, *"And ofttimes it hath cast him into the fire, and into the waters, to destroy him: but if thou canst do any thing, have compassion on us, and help us."* Notice the use of the pronouns. I do not have to tell any parent why the pronouns change. I do not have to tell anyone who has children why this man said to the Lord Jesus, "I love my boy. I have heard about all the things You can do, and I brought my boy to You. You were not here, so I brought him to the disciples in Your absence. You see, he has a dumb spirit. He wallows, foaming and gnashing at the teeth. Sometimes, he has been torn and thrown into the fire." No doubt, the boy was scarred in places because of the burns in the fire. Looking at his daddy, you would see scars on his body also. He, no doubt, had gone into the fire to rescue his son.

As the boy went into the waters, the father no doubt went into the waters after him like any father would. Perhaps on many occasions they were both almost drowned as the father saved the boy's life. He said, "Lord, maybe to others my son is unlovely and unwanted, but I love him. Help my son and help me. He has this dumb spirit, but have compassion on us." Why does he say, "Have compassion on us"? Because anytime someone you love is hurting, you are hurting with that person. If your daughter is ill and hurting, it makes no difference how old she is, you hurt with her. If your son is hurting, no matter what his age may be, you hurt with him.

The world is crying for someone to have compassion. We must reach the lost now, while a difference can be made.

God has put in our hands and in our hearts an ability to make a difference in people's lives. The reason we do not make the difference we could be making is that we are not caring. We are not caring like we could be caring. It is no wonder God says, *"Have compassion."*

I pray and ask God every day for wisdom because I believe that people who lead need special wisdom from God. If we read God's Word each day, the Lord will give us wisdom from His Word. He can also impart wisdom to help us make the right decisions through the indwelling Holy Spirit as we lean on Him. There are many men with knowledge but no wisdom. We need wisdom, the discernment to make right decisions.

When dealing with people, we also need compassion. Do you know who will make a difference in the lives of others? The people who care. It could be that the wrong kind of people care for them. The cry of the world is for someone to care for their souls. We must bring them to the Lord Jesus Christ.

The Compassion of Christ

Christ can change each of us into a caring person as we spend time with Him.

Christ is the greatest example of compassion. We are failing because of time not spent with Him. His passion becomes our passion only as we follow Him. It is impossible to care as Christ cares for lost souls unless we follow Him.

One of the most beautiful stories in the Bible about someone loving Christ is the story of Mary Magdalene. She was a demon-possessed woman living in the village of Magdala along the Sea of Galilee. The Lord Jesus saved her and made her whole. He cast the demons out. She stood at Calvary and watched Him bleed and die. She went to the garden tomb before anyone else arrived. She stayed after everyone else had gone. The Bible says in John 20:11-15,

> *But Mary stood without at the sepulchre weeping: and as she wept, she stooped down, and looked into the sepulchre, and seeth two angels in white sitting, the one at the head, and the other at the feet, where the body of Jesus had lain. And they say unto her, Woman, why weepest thou? She saith unto them, Because they have taken away my Lord, and I know not where they have laid him. And when she had thus said, she turned herself back, and saw Jesus standing, and knew not that it was Jesus. Jesus saith unto her, Woman, why weepest thou? whom seekest thou? She, supposing him to be the gardener, saith unto him, Sir, if thou have borne him hence, tell me where thou hast laid him, and I will take him away.*

The Lord Jesus asked Mary, *"Why are you weeping, and whom are you seeking?"* In other words, "What is wrong with you, and who can make it right?"

The Bible says that Christ spoke to her and called her by name. No one could speak her name like He could speak her name. When He spoke her name, she knew this was the Lord Jesus. Are we close enough to Christ to be able to care? Mary was a compassionate person because of her close fellowship with Christ. She loved Him for what He had done for her.

> *The reason we do not make the difference we could be making is that we are not caring.*

As God turns to His people, saying in Jude 20-21, *"But ye..."* He says we are to build ourselves up by reading God's Word. *"But ye, beloved, building up yourselves on your most holy faith, praying in the Holy Ghost. Keep yourselves in the love of God, looking for the mercy of our Lord Jesus Christ unto eternal life."*

It is no wonder that after God says, "Read My Word, spend time with Me in prayer, keep yourself in My love, and look for My return," the very next thing He says is *"have compassion."* God means for us to understand that we can spend time with Him in His Word, spend time with Him in prayer, spend time looking for and loving His return, and that will lead us into a fellowship with Christ that will produce compassion in our lives.

God's Word says that we are to make a difference. Salvation makes a difference. Witnessing and winning people to Christ makes a difference.

The Lord describes three distinct groups in Jude 23. Group one is the group that is brought to Christ through tenderly, lovingly giving the gospel over a period of time–*"and of some have compassion."*

Group two is the group that is close to hell. Our work must be done quickly–*"save with fear, pulling them out of the fire."* There is no time to waste.

Group three is the group that requires of the soul winner that he be very careful because of the sinful lifestyle the lost are living–*"hating even the garment spotted by the flesh."* We must prayerfully deal with these people to avoid hurting our testimonies while attempting to bring them to Christ.

What a joy to be used of God. There is no substitute for compassion. The love of Christ has conquered our hearts, and may His love be truly seen in us.

"Now unto him that is able to keep you from falling, and to present you faultless before the presence of his glory with exceeding joy, To the only wise God our Saviour, be glory and majesty, dominion and power, both now and ever. Amen."

Jude 24-25

CHAPTER THIRTEEN

HE IS ABLE

 e walk out of the book of Jude just as we walked into it–with a note of victory! God's people are victorious. One of the tremendous truths we must hold to in this hour of awful wickedness is the fact that we are victorious in the Lord Jesus Christ. Though at times it seems that the wicked are winning, God's people are on the victory side. Our Lord has conquered death, hell, and the grave. We are in Him, and He is in us. This means that all is well with God's people.

The book of Jude is about the age of the apostates, those who look at revealed truth and turn from it. There is no evidence in the Scripture to imply that it is possible for a Christian to become an apostate. We do not find this in the Bible, though we do find it in some men's thinking. We are born into God's family by the new birth, saved once and forever. We have everlasting life in Him. For the Christian, eternal life is not a hope for the future. It is a present possession.

The Bible says in Jude 24-25,

> *Now unto him that is able to keep you from falling, and to present you faultless before the presence of his glory with exceeding joy, to the only wise God our Saviour, be glory and majesty, dominion and power, both now and ever. Amen.*

Notice an expression found in the twenty-fourth verse, *"Unto him that is able."* God is able!

A dear man said to me recently, "I am afraid I will die and go to hell." I said, "Have you ever been saved? Do you know in your heart that you have trusted Jesus Christ as your personal Savior?" He said, "There is no doubt about it. I am trusting in Christ and Christ alone to get me to heaven." I said, "Friend, all your worry is unnecessary. You are safe in the arms of the Lord Jesus. There is no reason to worry or fear; God will keep His Word."

We are not able, but God is able.

In the twenty-fifth verse, the Bible says, *"To the only wise God our Saviour, be glory and majesty, dominion and power, both now and ever. Amen."* There is no darkness in Jesus Christ; there is only light. Think of His radiance, glory, majesty, dominion and power. He is King of Kings and Lord of Lords. His *"dominion"* refers to His reign. It is forever. The Word of God says, *"And power."* This refers to His right to be praised because He alone has prevailed.

The book of Jude serves as the hallway to the book of the Revelation of Jesus Christ. Throughout the book of the Revelation we move from earth to heaven and from heaven back to earth.

When we come to the fourth chapter of the Revelation, the church has been raptured. We will be gone from this world to be with the Lord Jesus forever. The world as we know it will not cease to exist. The lost world will enter into a period that is referred to as the Tribulation period. The Antichrist will make his appearance.

The Bible says in the fifth chapter of the Revelation of Jesus Christ that God is going to open a book. In that book we have represented to us all He has redeemed for His people and for this earth. In other words, God is going to unveil for us the future of the redeemed.

Have you ever thought about the way things should be? If things were the way they should be, Jesus Christ would be ruling and reigning upon the earth and everyone would be doing what is right. Is there no day coming when righteousness shall prevail in every quarter? There certainly is. We have that hope in the Lord. What a grand and glorious future we have because of what Jesus Christ has purchased for us!

The Bible says in the fifth chapter of the Revelation of Jesus Christ, verses one through three,

> *And I saw in the right hand of him that sat on the throne a book written within and on the backside, sealed with seven seals. And I saw a strong angel proclaiming with a loud voice, Who is worthy to open the book, and to loose the seals thereof? And no man in heaven, nor in earth, neither under the earth, was able to open the book, neither to look thereon.*

A number of books are mentioned in the Bible, such as the Lamb's Book of Life and the book of our works. Here is a book unveiling the future. The Lord says a strong angel calls out and his voice is heard in every area, in every realm, in heaven, in earth, and under the earth. He says, *"Who can open the book?"* In other words, "Who can bring about all that God has redeemed?" There is no answer. No man in heaven, no man in earth, and no man under the earth could answer. The Bible continues in verses four and five,

> *And I wept much, because no man was found worthy to open and to read the book, neither to look thereon. And one of the elders saith unto me, Weep not: behold, the Lion of the tribe of Juda, the Root of David, hath prevailed to open the book, and to loose the seven seals thereof.*

In verse four the weeping represents all the tears and suffering of humanity and the emptiness of every man's life if not redeemed. No wonder there is weeping. God speaks from heaven, *"Weep not: behold, the Lion of the tribe of Juda, the Root of David, hath prevailed."* What does He mean, *"Hath prevailed"*? He means that Christ came to earth and became a man without ceasing to be God,

> *When we are up against lions that try to ensnare us, God is able to deliver us.*

and not just a man, but obedient to the shameful, humiliating death of the cross. What does it mean that He has prevailed? It means that He lived a sinless life; that nothing kept Him from going to Calvary to bleed and die for our sins; that He tasted death for every man. It means that He was buried in a borrowed tomb and on the third day the grave was empty because He came forth bodily alive forevermore. No wonder the Bible says that He *"hath prevailed."* To Him *"be glory and majesty, dominion and power, both now and ever. Amen."* This is the wonderful Savior that we know and love. This is our Lord Jesus!

When we walk through the book of Jude, through the apostates, and we read of all the terrible things that are going on under the guise of religion, God knows that our hearts are heavy. God knows that sometimes we get weary in it all. No wonder He closes the book by saying, *"He is able!"* To Him is *"glory and majesty, dominion and power, both now and ever. Amen."*

He is able. This is the message that needs to be heard in this day and hour. There is so much weakness, so much fainting, and so many people who are downcast and discouraged. The message is *"He is able."* This is the message that we need to be preaching and the message that we need to be living. Consider some of the things He is able to do.

ABLE TO DELIVER

In the sixth chapter of Daniel, Daniel was faithfully serving the Lord, and because of his faith in God he was going to be cast into a den of lions. The Bible says in Daniel 6:16-24,

> *Then the king commanded, and they brought Daniel, and cast him into the den of lions. Now the king spake and said unto Daniel, Thy God whom thou servest continually, he will deliver thee. And a stone was brought, and laid upon the mouth of the den; and the king sealed it with his own signet, and with the signet of his lords; that the purpose might not be changed concerning Daniel. Then the king went to his palace, and passed the night fasting: neither were instruments of musick brought before him: and his sleep went from him. Then the king arose*

_very early in the morning, and went in haste unto
the den of lions. And when he came to the den,
he cried with a lamentable voice unto Daniel:
and the king spake and said to Daniel...._

Can you imagine this scene? Daniel, because of his faith in God, had been thrown into a den of hungry lions. The king had spent a sleepless night, and he went in haste the next morning and _"with a lamentable voice"_ called out to Daniel,

_O Daniel, servant of the living God, is thy
God, whom thou servest continually, able to
deliver thee from the lions? Then said Daniel
unto the king, O king, live for ever. My God hath
sent his angel, and hath shut the lions' mouths,
that they have not hurt me: forasmuch as before
him innocency was found in me; and also before
thee, O king, have I done no hurt. Then was the
king exceeding glad for him, and commanded
that they should take Daniel up out of the den.
So Daniel was taken up out of the den, and no
manner of hurt was found upon him, because he
believed in his God. And the king commanded,
and they brought those men which had accused
Daniel, and they cast them into the den of lions,
them, their children, and their wives; and the
lions had the mastery of them, and brake all
their bones in pieces or ever they came at the
bottom of the den._

God's Word said that before the accusers of Daniel reached the bottom of the den of lions, all their bones were broken in pieces. Is God able? Ask Daniel. He would tell you that God is able to deliver. When we are up against lions that try to ensnare us, God is able to deliver us.

Able to Make Grace Abound

The Bible says in II Corinthians 9:8, *"And God is able to make all grace abound toward you."* Not only is He able, but He is able to make all grace abound. This means He has more than we need. For whatever we face, God is able to give us grace.

Able to Do Exceeding Abundantly Above

The Bible says in Ephesians 3:20, *"Now unto him that is able to do exceeding abundantly above all that we ask or think, according to the power that worketh in us."* Some people consider themselves to be big thinkers and big dreamers. The Bible says that our God is able to do more than we can even think. God is *"able to do exceeding abundantly above all that we ask or think."*

Able to Subdue All Things

The Bible says in Philippians 3:21, *"Who shall change our vile body, that it may be fashioned like unto his glorious body, according to the working whereby he is able even to subdue all things unto himself."* He is able to subdue all things unto Himself.

God's people can have a strong assurance in their hearts that all is well because the Lord Jesus is able to subdue all things under His feet. God is able.

Able to Save to the Uttermost

The Bible says in Hebrews 7:25, *"Wherefore he is able also to save them to the uttermost that come unto God by him."*

Think about the most hardened sinner you know–God is able to save him. God is able.

In Jude1-2 the Bible says,

> *Jude, the servant of Jesus Christ, and brother of James, to them that are sanctified by God the Father, and preserved in Jesus Christ, and called: Mercy unto you, and peace, and love, be multiplied.*

In verse three God's Word says,

> *Beloved, when I gave all diligence to write unto you of the common salvation, it was needful for me to write unto you, and exhort you that ye should earnestly contend for the faith which was once delivered unto the saints.*

In the fourth verse God says,

> *For there are certain men crept in unawares, who were before of old ordained to this condemnation, ungodly men, turning the grace of our God into lasciviousness, and denying the only Lord God, and our Lord Jesus Christ.*

Look at the examples God gives us in verses five through seven,

> *I will therefore put you in remembrance, though ye once knew this, how that the Lord, having saved the people out of the land of Egypt, afterward destroyed them that believed not. And the angels which kept not their first estate, but left their own habitation, he hath reserved in everlasting chains under darkness unto the judgment of the great day. Even as Sodom and Gomorrha, and the cities about them in like*

manner, giving themselves over to fornication, and going after strange flesh, are set forth for an example, suffering the vengeance of eternal fire.

In verses eight and nine the Lord says,

Likewise also these filthy dreamers defile the flesh, despise dominion, and speak evil of dignities. Yet Michael the archangel, when contending with the devil he disputed about the body of Moses, durst not bring against him a railing accusation, but said, The Lord rebuke thee.

Look again at the crowd in verses ten through sixteen,

But these speak evil of those things which they know not: but what they know naturally, as brute beasts, in those things they corrupt themselves. Woe unto them! for they have gone in the way of Cain, and ran greedily after the error of Balaam for reward, and perished in the gainsaying of Core. These are spots in your feasts of charity, when they feast with you, feeding themselves without fear: clouds they are without water, carried about of winds; trees whose fruit withereth, without fruit, twice dead, plucked up by the roots; raging waves of the sea, foaming out their own shame; wandering stars, to whom is reserved the

> *We not only have final victory, but we have victory through faith in Christ on a daily basis.*

blackness of darkness for ever. And Enoch also, the seventh from Adam, prophesied of these, saying, Behold, the Lord cometh with ten thousands of his saints, To execute judgment upon all, and to convince all that are ungodly among them of all their ungodly deeds which they have ungodly committed, and of all their hard speeches which ungodly sinners have spoken against him. These are murmurers, complainers, walking after their own lusts; and their mouth speaketh great swelling words, having men's persons in admiration because of advantage.

In this age of apostasy, it is wonderful to know that God is able.

HE IS ABLE TO KEEP YOU FROM FALLING

"He is able to keep you from falling." What does this mean? It means that we never have to worry about going to hell if we have been saved. He keeps us from falling. The Lord Jesus said in John 10:27-29,

> *My sheep hear my voice, and I know them, and they follow me: and I give unto them eternal life; and they shall never perish, neither shall any man pluck them out of my hand. My Father, which gave them me, is greater than all; and no man is able to pluck them out of my Father's hand.*

No wonder the Bible says that He is able to keep us from falling. Did you know that He is standing guard over us? I did not save myself. I asked the Lord to forgive my sin, and by faith

I received Jesus Christ as my Savior. We all deserve to die and go to hell. We did not save ourselves; God saved us.

The Bible says in Hebrews 7:25 that *"he ever liveth to make intercession for them."* This means that every moment of our lives, now that we are God's children, Jesus Christ keeps us saved. He keeps us from falling. I have sinned, and I have sought my heavenly Father's forgiveness, but I do not have to worry about dying and going to hell. Think of the poor people who have to wonder, going under a surgeon's knife, about dying on the operating table and going to hell. Think about people who are overcome with the thought of getting into an automobile and being killed in an accident, of dying and going to hell. We not only have final victory, but we have victory through faith in Christ on a daily basis.

HE IS ABLE TO PRESENT YOU FAULTLESS

It will be a great day when He presents us faultless. Those of us who are saved have been washed in the blood of Christ and are counted righteous before God each moment. Can you imagine being perfect?

There has only been one truly faultless person who ever lived—the Son of God. No wonder Pilate said in His trial, *"I find no fault in Him."*

Can you imagine with all our problems that the Bible says there is coming a day when God is going to present us faultless? What a day! We do not have to worry about what we are going to wear that day. God is going to clothe us.

EARNESTLY CONTEND FOR THE FAITH

The Bible says in Ephesians 5:25-27,

> *Husbands, love your wives, even as Christ also loved the church, and gave himself for it; that he might sanctify and cleanse it with the washing of water by the word, that he might present it to himself a glorious church, not having spot, or wrinkle, or any such thing; but that it should be holy and without blemish.*

We cannot get rid of the blemishes here, but God says some day all the blemishes will be gone. He is able to present us faultless.

We will never really be able to fully understand with our finite minds what Jesus Christ did for us on the cross. We believe it, but we cannot comprehend the depth of it. There is coming a day when God, our heavenly Father, will present us to Jesus Christ, our heavenly Groom, and say, "Here is the bride, faultless."

> *There is coming a day when God, our heavenly Father, will present us to Jesus Christ, our heavenly Groom, and say, "Here is the bride, faultless."*

God is able. Some day I will lay down this robe of flesh and soar beyond the stars. Some day I will say goodbye to every heartache and sorrow. Some day I will step on a street of gold and look in the face of the Lord Jesus. When I do, I will be perfect. I will behold Him in all His glory. I will be able to do so because I will be like Him when I see Him as He is. He is able!

190

The concluding word in this epistle is *"amen."* These words are true; these words are faithful. Every believer in the Lord Jesus Christ will come to this conclusion. The conclusion is *"amen."* These solemn warnings have been set forth by God to instruct us and inspire us in these perilous times. One of the titles for Christ is *"the Amen."* We are complete in Him. Our victory is in Him. As God's people, we can say, *"Amen."*

THE STORY OF HUGH LATIMER

ecently while travelling in England with a group of people from our church, I had the privilege of standing on the spot where Latimer and Ridley were put to death for their faith. The following is an account of Latimer's death:

And so at length came the morning, October 16, 1555, when Latimer was led forth out of Oxford jail to die with his younger companion Ridley. The bent and feeble old man hobbled along in his old frieze coat, crying to his comrade, 'Have after you as fast as I can follow,' and so they came to the open space beyond Balliol College. Then Ridley embraced his friend, and they kneeled down there and prayed together, and then, stripping off their outer clothes and giving little remembrances to their friends, they were ready for the fire.

'Before,' says Foxe, speaking of Latimer, 'he appeared a withered and crooked old man,' but as the keeper pulled off his dress and left him standing in his shroud, he now stood bolt upright, as comely a father as one would wish to see.

Mercifully, a friend hung a bag of gun-powder round the neck of each of them, and then they were chained back to back to the post, and the fire was brought. 'Play the man, Master Ridley,' said Latimer as the gorse below the faggots kindled and crackled; 'We shall this day light such a candle by God's grace in England, as I trust shall never be put out,' and as the flames rose up, he bathed his hands in them, as it were, until they reached the powder, and he died.

THE STORY OF LADY JANE GREY

n Leicestershire a few miles north of Leicester is Bradgate Park. A winding path leads through a beautiful park passing historic trees. Those trees once witnessed the playfulness of two little girls. One was Jane Grey, who lived with her parents at the mansion situated at the end of the path. The other girl was Elizabeth, in later years, Queen Elizabeth I of England.

Elizabeth would, on occasion, visit the Grey family to play with Jane. The Grey family was of royal stock, an honor to be cherished, but for Jane–a curse–ending her life at age sixteen.

Jane was an amazingly gifted and highly educated young woman. By the age of eleven, she was corresponding with leaders of the reformation in continental Europe. (Those letters still exist in Switzerland.) The tragic death of Jane Grey resulted from a power play for the throne of England.

Parliament had authorized King Henry VIII to nominate his successor to the throne. He had selected his two daughters Mary and Elizabeth to succeed him, if his son Edward left no heirs. Should these three rule and die without heirs, a remote possibility, Henry directed that the throne would then pass to the family of his younger sister (another Mary).

This younger sister had died leaving two daughters, Jane Grey being the younger. Hence Jane Grey could become legal queen only if Edward, Henry's son, and Mary and Elizabeth all died without heirs.

During the early part of 1553, King Edward, then only fifteen years old, was dying. Upon his death, the next in line of succession was Mary, a passionate Catholic. The Duke of Northumberland, a devout Protestant, initiated a play to bypass Mary, the legal heir to the throne and in her place to install Jane as queen. Part of Northumberland's plan included Jane marrying his son. This marriage took place with the complicity of her parents but against her own will.

As the plot unfolded, an attempt to capture Mary failed. Being forewarned, she fled to Norfolk gaining time to appeal for help. Told of her succession, Lady Jane Grey protested. She had little desire to occupy the throne at the Tower of London. Her parents insisted. The circle of leaders surrounding her shamed her should she not rise to save England by becoming queen.

For nine days, Jane and her husband occupied the state apartment at the Tower. Meanwhile the scheme to replace Mary was parting at the seams. A force, led by Northumberland, to capture Mary at Norfolk had failed. The country at large knew very little of Jane Grey. Mary they knew as the legal successor to the throne. Jane was looked upon as a usurper. With all opposing forces in disarray, Mary entered London in early August with popular support.

Betrayed, Jane now found herself deserted by those who had forced her to become queen. It was now apparent that their chief motive had been their own political position. Her own father, seeing the unfolding of events, did an about face and proclaimed Mary as queen. He returned to the Tower and found his daughter sitting, bewildered, on the throne, in the council chamber. "Come down from there, my child...that is no place for you." He then explained to her that she was no longer queen. She looked at him and in all the innocence of a sixteen-year-old girl asked, "Can I go home now?" The young girl was escorted from the chamber to another, although comfortable, quarters, now the prisoner of Mary.

Queen Mary realized that Jane had been used. She was fond of Jane and planned to release her. Being a close relative, Mary had known Jane all of her life. She secretly sent a message to Jane saying that a pardon would be granted at an appropriate time. However, the political stage demanded another course.

Mary desired to re-establish Catholicism in England. Being surrounded by Papal advisors and facing strong Protestant revolt, she now found Jane Grey a serious liability. She could not now be set free without her becoming a figurehead for the opposition. There was a way out for Mary. If she could persuade Jane to renounce the Protestant faith and become a Catholic, then release would be possible. This act would immediately disqualify Jane in the eyes of the Reformers, as a leader.

Jane, however, would not deny her faith. Everyone around her, Protestant and Catholic, was guilty of religious politics. Jane had watched them use religious symbols to gain personal ends. Jane, however, caught up and used in their "web of deceit," was too pure to deny truth.

Queen Mary's next step was to involve Jane in a public debate in the Tower. Perhaps the Papal advisors could persuade her that she was wrong. *Foxe's Book of Martyrs* records this event. Lady Jane Grey was no mere uneducated country girl. She defended the Protestant faith with a clarity so profound that her opponents were left speechless.

The debate ended with the young woman standing head and shoulders above the Roman debaters. Queen Mary now saw Jane as a major threat to her throne. Jane Grey's innocence, her friendship with Mary in past days, now all faded into nothing. "Political correctness" would rule.

There was only one avenue left to Mary and that was to remove Jane Grey permanently from the stage...by death.

On February 12, 1554, Lady Jane Grey went to the block in the Tower of London proclaiming the message of Christ. The night before she died, she sent her sister Katherine a copy of the Greek Testament urging her to read it.

> It shall teach you to live, and learn you to die. It
> shall win you more than you should have gained
> by the possession of your woeful father's lands.

From her window, Jane saw her young husband being led away to execution. From that same window later she saw his headless body being brought back in a cart. She exclaimed,

Oh, Guildford, the pain you have tasted, and I shall soon taste, is nothing to the feast you and I shall partake of this day in Paradise.

Then Jane herself was led out, a small sandy-haired girl dressed in a gown and a velvet cover on her head. Her last words were:

Good people—I am come here to die...I wash my hands in innocence, before God. Bear witness that I die a true Christian woman, and that I look to be saved by none other means, but only by the mercy of God in the merits of the blood of His only Son Jesus Christ. I thank God for His goodness that He hath thus given me a time to repent. While I am alive, assist me with your prayers.

Then she quoted a psalm before handing her gloves and handkerchief to her maid. The brutal executioner was shaken. He was not prepared for this. He was used to victims cursing and resisting, but this was a beautiful young Christian woman, gentle and innocent and only sixteen years old. She could have been his daughter. "Forgive me" he begged her. Jane replied, "You are forgiven. Do your work quickly."

She then tied the handkerchief over her eyes. Putting her hands out she could not feel the block and cried out, "Where is it? What shall I do?" An onlooker helped her to find the block, on which she laid her head, saying, "Lord, into Thy hands I commend my spirit."

In Leicestershire there still stands the church where Jane Grey attended as a girl. Down the path leading from the church lies the ruins of the Grey family home where Jane was born in 1537. In the grounds of the Tower of London lies the block upon which she placed her head after a profound testimony for Jesus Christ. Lady Jane Grey is mentioned in the *Guinness Book of Records* as the first sovereign queen of England.

Lady Jane Grey, if not the greatest, must surely take her place as one of the "purest" martyrs who ever lived and died for Jesus Christ.

By James Ray
European Director, Baptist International Missions, Inc.
(Reprinted by Permission)

Sunday School materials are available for use in conjunction with *Earnestly Contend For the Faith*. For a complete listing of available materials from Crown Christian Publications, please call 1-877 AT CROWN, or write to: 1700 Beaver Creek Drive ♦ Powell, TN 37849

Visit us on the Web at FaithfortheFamily.com
"A Website for the Christian Family"

CROWN
CHRISTIAN
PUBLICATIONS
Royal Reading

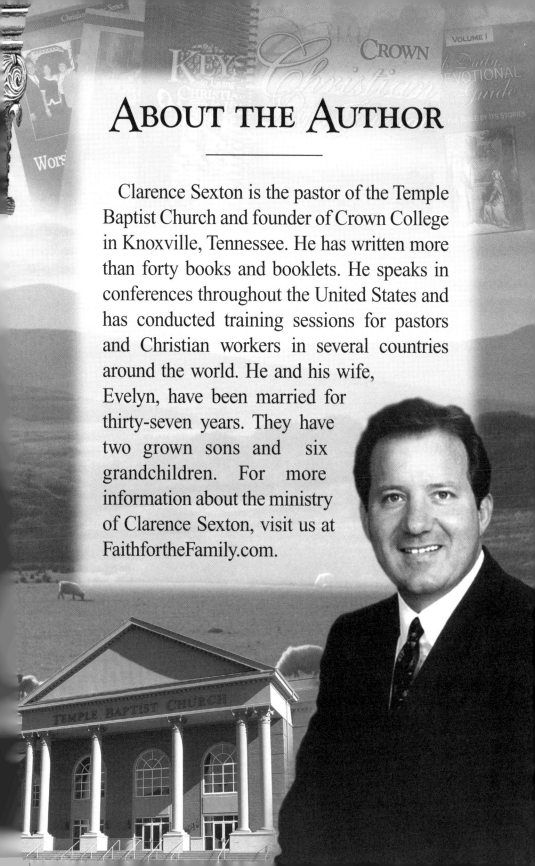

ABOUT THE AUTHOR

Clarence Sexton is the pastor of the Temple
Baptist Church and founder of Crown College
in Knoxville, Tennessee. He has written more
than forty books and booklets. He speaks in
conferences throughout the United States and
has conducted training sessions for pastors
and Christian workers in several countries
around the world. He and his wife,
Evelyn, have been married for
thirty-seven years. They have
two grown sons and   six
grandchildren.   For   more
information about the ministry
of Clarence Sexton, visit us at
FaithfortheFamily.com.